GEOFFREY HOWE

A Quiet Revolutionary

GEOFFREY HOWE
A Quiet Revolutionary

Judy Hillman
and
Peter Clarke

WEIDENFELD AND NICOLSON
LONDON

PICTURE ACKNOWLEDGEMENTS

The photographs in this book were provided by Sir Geoffrey Howe except for the following:

Daily Mail (1.3); Judy Hillman (2.5, 2.15); *The Financial Times* (2.2, 2.3, 2.4); Miss Enid John (1.3); Mr Ron Needs (1.7); Press Association (2.11); Tass (2.12); *The Times* (2.14 and 2.14A); Mrs Jennifer Wakelin (1.12).

Published in Great Britain by
George Weidenfeld & Nicolson Limited
91 Clapham High Street
London SW4 7TA

Printed in Great Britain by The Bath Press, Avon

Contents

Introduction

Sir Geoffrey Howe has fashioned some of the most crucial reforms of our society. He first brought the trade unions back within the law. He is the man who guided the necessary legislation through the House of Commons for Britain to join the European Community.

As Chancellor of the Exchequer Geoffrey Howe brought public expenditure under greater control and reduced inflation, confounding former Keynesian practice and expectations. Through the courageous abolition of exchange control he allowed individuals to buy and sell property abroad without hindrance and, much more important, enabled British companies to invest overseas and create an enormous new source of income. As Foreign Secretary he has been able to transmit the confidence born from renewed economic vitality and restore Britain's role on a world stage.

With four major offices of state under his belt, it is curious that until recently many people have tended to overlook Geoffrey Howe's potential as a candidate for the highest office. He is known as a nice man, whose head has hardly ever risen above the political parapet. Yet there undoubtedly lurks a steely ambition within the affable exterior, which continued criticism of his parliamentary style has failed to deter. Outside Westminster in the Tory Party he has always been a popular speaker, but his quiet, modest approach has obscured the sharp radicalism of his ideas.

He may lack the flamboyance of a Palmerston-type figure, for example. But it was this combination of obvious ability, reforming zeal and lack of general public recognition which made us think of writing his biography. It is bound to be partial and incomplete, as is any book written about someone who is alive with unfulfilled ambitions and potential. A real assessment of Sir Geoffrey Howe will have to wait for future generations, who will have the advantage of knowing when and where he stopped. For the moment, this is simply a contemporary attempt, with the limitations that involves, to understand something of the man, his ideas and achievements.

Sir Geoffrey will hopefully one day write his memoirs. But, while this is in no sense an authorized biography, both he and Lady Howe have spared time for a number of interviews and provided archive material such as speeches and pamphlets, for which we are most grateful. However, it is our story and our interpretation.

A great number of other people, friends from Parliament, the Bow Group, Cambridge, the army, Winchester and Wales have helped with this story. Many have spoken on a non-attributable basis and, rather than list only those who have felt able to allow themselves to be quoted, which should become obvious from the text, we would like simply to thank everyone very much indeed. Without their generous assistance, it would have been very difficult even to begin to understand this popular, but private, man.

However, there are two people whom we feel should nevertheless have special mention. The first, Colin Howe, Geoffrey's younger brother, died early in 1988. Although he was not at all well, he made time and the effort in October to meet Judy Hillman at King's College Hospital, where he had been a surgeon and was still lecturing. He came armed with a photograph of the Howe parents with Lloyd George in full flowing cloak. The conversation mainly concerned the period when the two brothers were growing up in Wales. The second, Stephen Abbot, died in 1987. He worked with Geoffrey Howe on the Industrial Relations Bill and spent the best part of a day in the summer talking to Peter Clarke at his home in Hampshire.

We would also like to thank the Bow Group for access to *Crossbow* files and members of staff at the Westminster central reference library for unfailing help and courtesy.

Judy Hillman has known Sir Geoffrey as a friend since she worked with him on *Crossbow*, the Bow Group quarterly. Peter Clarke particularly admired him for the abolition of exchange control. Very broadly Judy Hillman has covered his career up to 1970 and his years at the Foreign Office, and Peter Clarke has concentrated on the period when he was first in government as Solicitor-General and Minister for Trade and Consumer Affairs, then in Opposition and finally in the key role in the Thatcher Government as Chancellor of the Exchequer.

Judy Hillman
Peter Clarke

February 1988

Kingdom Come

A knyght ther was, Sir Geoffrye was his name,
Who since the tymme from dystant Wales he came,
   He never yet no villeynye had sayde.
Though in his bearing, modest as a mayde
He'd fought his Lady's cause with all his myte.
   He was a verray parfit, gentil, knyght.

Henry Stanhope, *The Times*, 29 September 1987

'Our Father, which art in heaven, hallowed be Thy name,
Thy kingdom come ...' As Sir Geoffrey Howe stepped out
of the official British embassy limousine into the April night
air, the crowd of some eight or nine hundred Poles, who had
got wind of his visit and gathered at the churchyard of St
Stanislaw Kostka in Warsaw, began to chant the words of
the Lord's Prayer, then sing the Polish national anthem. Flam-
ing torches lent an almost timeless quality to the scene as
a little blonde girl presented flowers of red and white, the
Polish national colours. Then the mass of people crying 'Vive
Anglia' propelled the British Foreign Secretary forward to the
grave of Father Jerzy Popeluszko, the priest who had been
murdered by the secret police, where he quietly laid the flowers
and lit a candle for freedom. A calculated snub designed to
emphasize the British Government's support for the ideals of
'Solidarity', Sir Geoffrey's unofficial post-cocktails engagement

1

was almost unbearably moving and a symbolic climax to a highly successful trip to Eastern Europe.

Only two nights before he had been joyously singing *Good King Wenceslas* and the Welsh hymn *Bread of Heaven* in the Seven Angels gypsy tavern in Prague with his Czechoslovakian opposite number, numerous officials and members of the press. Luckily, no one, not even the British press, understood or, if they did, recognized the significance of the choice as the Foreign Secretary sang *Cwm Rhondda*, which in English would have been: 'Guide us, O Thou Great Redeemer, pilgrims through this barren land.' Equally, neither hosts nor reporters knew that two senior Foreign Office officials had quietly, during this celebration, achieved a rendezvous with representatives of the dissident Charter 77 Group to discuss abuses of human rights. Eight months later in a speech to the Royal College of Defence Studies in London, Sir Geoffrey was to admit that this occasion was the closest he had come to the sort of spontaneous joy experienced by Monșieur Spaak who, after the signing of the treaty to set up the European Community, burst into *O Sole Mio* at 4 am on the castle ramparts at Taormina. Ever diplomatic, the Foreign Secretary then quickly denied there had been any form of 'cunning choral plot' to distract the Czechoslovakian Foreign Minister while 'terrible skulduggery' took place elsewhere.

Skulduggery or skilful planning, contact had been made and the British Foreign Minister had himself seen the Czech cardinal, East German Protestants and, in Berlin, sounded a trumpet call to bring down all the walls and barriers which still divide people. *Le Monde* summed up his trip as affecting the case for human rights in 'a spectacular fashion'. Meanwhile the London *Times'* main leader column declared that it was the first time a British Foreign Secretary, let alone a European foreign minister, had made it abundantly clear that any serious improvement in arms control and economic development with the Soviet bloc depended fundamentally on advances in human freedoms within that system. 'Sir Geoffrey has sounded the first note on the trumpet. Will others follow?' it asked. According to *The Observer*, he had, on his brief tour of Eastern Europe, shown 'considerable – and to some, previously unsuspected – political skills ... On last week's showing she (Mrs

Thatcher) would be well advised to stay at home and leave foreign policy to Sir Geoffrey.' Perhaps the last word should be left to PHS in the then *Times* diary: 'Who says he is Mogadon man?'

1

A Welsh Childhood

Geoffrey Howe was born in Port Talbot, South Wales, on 20 December 1926, the year of the General Strike. All births are near miracles to their parents but the arrival of this baby was all the more important in that Barbara, the little girl who would have been his elder sister, had died a few months earlier of meningitis. Any child born into this situation will be all the more cherished, but can never quite compensate for the one who is lost.

The Howe background was solidly comfortable, professional middle class in a primarily working-class community in which his parents won prominence and respect. Ambitious for their two sons – Colin was born in 1929 – they not merely departed from family precedent and raised their sights to public school education but decided on Winchester, Britain's premier intellectual training ground and springboard for a professional, academic or ecclesiastical career well away from the then coal and steel economy of South Wales.

Geoffrey's father, Edward, or Eddie to his friends, was a solicitor who became a partner in his uncle's Port Talbot practice and later county coroner and Clerk to the Justices. Born in 1889, he was a big, heavy man, very Welsh, a Freemason and some seven years older than his wife, whom he courted in Llandrindod Wells and married in 1922. Christened Eliza Florence Thomson, she was known by everyone as Lili (to rhyme with Smiley). That was the name used on her wedding invitation and on the commemoration stone many years later when she opened the new local county court.

Mrs Howe was beautiful and, together with her identical twin sister Peggy, one of the belles of Cardiff society. Her father, the son of a Scottish crofter, became a grocer's boy in Liverpool, finally setting up a chain of about thirty-five grocery shops in South Wales known as the Direct Trading Company. Lili, herself born in Liverpool, went to grammar school and, while highly intelligent, was free from blue-stocking pretensions, preferring to sparkle in the local social limelight. Her personality was magnetic, she loved people, was delightful company herself and exuded a natural glamour which was to remain throughout her life. In the 1920s in Cardiff it was the custom for the younger generation to don their most fashionable outfits and go into the city on Saturday mornings to see and be seen, and generally meet their contemporaries. The good-looking Thomson twins would join in, sometimes carrying small dogs under their arms. They also delighted in confusing friends and acquaintances about their respective identities. Once, when the doctor confined Lili to bed with a bad attack of influenza, he then arrived to find her sitting in her bedroom in a dressing-gown. On solemnly berating her for her foolishness, the real Lili suddenly popped up from under the sheets and blankets on the bed, where she had been all the time.

Lili Thomson married Edward Howe when she was twenty-six and he was thirty-three. Like so many marriages, it is impossible to fathom the chemistry of attraction between this charismatic young woman and the Port Talbot solicitor. But for him she must have provided light and laughter – and some substance. For her there may have been the prospect of stability and social advance. Although the lack of class subservience is a positive Welsh virtue, it was still a time when trade looked up to the professions.

In any event, the Howes quickly became key members of Port Talbot society making friends and, until the war, leading a typically comfortable and enjoyable life. The town, which focused on tin-plate manufacture and coal exports through the docks, had a population of about 40,000 compared with 50,000 today. The family lived first in Penycae and then moved to a house called *Rockleigh* in Pentyla; a large, semi-detached, Edwardian gothic property. Set on the side of a hill and backing immediately onto steep moorland, the garden fronted the main road from Cardiff (through Port Talbot and Baglan) to Swansea, now replaced by the M4. The south-facing windows then looked towards the silver-grey Bristol Channel over grass and sand dunes. Nowadays the low-lying ground is blanketed by streets of identikit red-brick housing built to serve the massive steelworks, which dominate this part of the shore. After the Second World War, Marshall Aid money was used to take advantage of local iron and coal and help eradicate the ingrained memories of the 1930s – the lack of work, the dole queue, boarded-up shops and gaunt poverty, which provided the backcloth to Geoffrey's childhood.

While the misery of the Depression was all too obvious, at that time the tradition of domestic service extended well beyond the aristocracy and upper middle class to provide one of the few avenues by which poor members of the British working class could escape the extremes of poverty and the appalling dietary norm of tea, bread, margarine and potatoes. As part of an established household, a cook or maid might earn as much as £75 a year on top of regular meals, uniform and a warm roof over her head.

The Howes were no different from their contemporaries in professional life and had at different times a maid; a nanny, who would nowadays be called a mother's help; someone who worked in the garden and a driver. As with similar families all over Britain, this left Mrs Howe with time to play the piano and to garden, which she loved, and to have a very full social life – not grand but entertaining and fun; often dinner and bridge (black tie was the norm) and centred around the local golf club. This was Mr Howe's sport, not perhaps in terms of natural flair but as a healthy means of pushing into the background the worries of a perforce depressing role as coronor dealing with accidental and unexplained death. The two Howe boys would frequently act as caddies.

In addition, the parents were regular supporters of Welsh rugby football at Cardiff Arms Park, and further afield. When the parents were away, Geoffrey and Colin would stay with their Auntie Lil, Mr Howe's sister Elizabeth; a large, kind, serious, motherly woman, headmistress of the local infants school, who got on extremely well with her sister-in-law and was devoted to her nephews. Pineapple chunks, at 4d a tin, were the favourite for tea. An understanding aunt, who stands just outside the immediate tensions of normal family life, is a boon to any child and her devotion was returned, particularly by the young Geoffrey. All five would holiday at Le Coq-sur-Mer in Belgium, when very few families travelled regularly abroad and, at a later stage, following her retirement, Auntie Lil moved in with the Howe parents and took over the family cooking. By then servants were pre-war memories and Mrs Howe had abandoned the social round for voluntary service in the local community including, as a magistrate, deputy chairmanship of the local bench.

Miss Enid John, now in her eighties, a former friend of the Howes and still living near *Rockleigh*, remembers the Howe boys as children. 'When Geoffrey was a little boy and their cat was going to have kittens, Lili had a box in the garage and Geoffrey was very cross. "You didn't have to go in the garage to have us," he stormed at his mother.'

The Howe boys were, to use Miss John's phrase, naughty children, although nowadays the description would probably be high spirited. They even played up one maid, Lizzie, so much that she threatened to leave if they did not stop. Of course, they carried on and she pretended to keep her word. They telephoned their father to say she had gone and that they were alone in the house. Mr Howe, as coroner, was all too well aware of the ease with which accidents can happen and had impressed on them the need for care. It was a memorable day.

Geoffrey was more serious than his brother; Colin then had more of his mother's instinctive charm. Miss John recalls: 'She used to say to me, "Now we're telling you, we're not telling anyone else" and point her finger like that. I remember her saying, "Geoffrey is bringing a girl down" in a low secretive voice. I went over to see this girl. She was very young but quiet composed and calm.' That was Elspeth, Geoffrey's wife and now Lady Howe.

The family was non-conformist, Geoffrey's father attending Carmel, a Welsh Methodist church with services in Welsh, his mother a Presbyterian establishment called Bethany. Miss John remembers the young boys playing chapel and Geoffrey was always the preacher.

Of course there were friends and fun outside as well, in particular with the Jenkins sisters, Ruth and Margaret, whose parents remained great friends of Mr and Mrs Howe after they moved to the north west of England. The Jenkins girls went to Roedean, when the school was evacuated to Keswick, but they would come back to Porthcawl for holidays, where the Howes sometimes rented a house on the promenade and the two boys would cycle over for picnics and cricket games on the sands. There were also occasions when a group of Port Talbot boys would actually be allowed into the engine to drive the tiny local train which linked the seaside town with the mainline junction at Pyle.

But basic family ambition and typical Welsh confidence in the virtues and advantages of education set the pattern for the future. Miss John continues: 'G's got a great deal to thank his father for because he was determined he was going to Winchester. He looked up all the schools that would take both boys there. Eddie was bright himself and had a very bright uncle and probably Geoffrey gets his brains from him. Geoffrey had better brains than people give him credit for. He's brilliant but he doesn't show it.'

Certainly Geoffrey's great uncle, Edward T. Evans, whose sister Hannah married his grandfather, was almost a local intellectual folk hero. He started off life as an office boy, moved to a firm of solicitors, took articles, qualified, left to become deputy town clerk of Aberavon and then set up his own legal practice. In the meantime, self-taught, he achieved a first class honours degree in law. He could also speak French, German, Latin, Greek and Hebrew, was a classical Welsh scholar, helped found the chapels at Carmel and Bethany, conducted the Male Voice Party, including at the National Eisteddfod, and served as a Liberal on both the local district and Glamorgan County Councils. Although he died in 1912, well before Geoffrey was born, Great Uncle 'E.T.' was not forgotten but a key component of the Howe family mythology.

Geoffrey's grandfather, a senior deacon and yet another Edward, was also elected as a Liberal to Margam District

Council and was one of the founders of the Tin-platers's Union. As coroner, Geoffrey's father, the third Edward, stood aside from party politics but took a keen interest in matters of the day. Certainly politics, public service and the law, combined with a liberal outlook, formed part of the natural inheritance of the young Richard Edward Geoffrey Howe.

Indeed, liberalism was sufficiently strong for Geoffrey, in July 1945 soon after leaving school, to canvass for the local Liberal candidate in Exeter where he was on a short university course as a preliminary to his national service in the Royal Signals. However, by the time he returned to take up his scholarship to study law at Cambridge in 1948, he had decided that the post-war Tory Party was the party of his brand of liberalism and his proper political home. Concerned about the rights and responsibilities of individuals, he has contributed at least as much, if not more, than any other contemporary politician to the development of modern Conservative policy and its implementation in government. But that is moving ahead in time.

Geoffrey went to a series of schools, first his aunt's, then a little private school in Port Talbot; and then as a day boy at Bryntirion, a preparatory school just outside Bridgend with about sixty boys, most of whom were boarders. 'I can see myself looking at a revolving front door of this prep school watching Geoffrey and his brother taking the car – the driver used to turn up each afternoon,' says Huw Thomas, a contemporary, who also later became a barrister, then an Independent Television newcaster and now runs his own corporate affairs consultancy. 'I felt terribly homesick. To be able to go home and not have to put up with dormitories.' Their friendship really grew later when they met again at Cambridge, although they were in different colleges and belonged to different political associations. Huw Thomas did become a Liberal.

Most Bryntirion boys went on to minor public schools. However Geoffrey, on reaching the top form by the age of eleven, was sent in 1938 to Abberley Hall, Worcestershire, to prepare for the scholarship examinations for Winchester. Run by one of the legendary Ashton cricketing brothers, Gilbert, the school, an expensive springboard for Eton and Winchester, provided a tough training ground with tiny classes, endless tests and competitive boxing. Latin, Greek, French, English, divinity, history, geography and mathematics formed the main diet in this élite forcing house. In spite of its intellectual bias, there was still some time for the piano and playing in the band, and the young Howe, according to one school report, even showed some promise as a forward in rugger. By the summer of 1940 Geoffrey, his Welsh accent still more or less intact, came sixteenth on the Winchester roll (then considered slightly more difficult than Eton) missing a scholarship by four places but winning an exhibition and, more important since money was not a problem, a place in one of Britain's most famous public schools. His brother Colin, who later became a surgeon, followed him to Abberley Hall and also went on to Winchester but into a different house. Partly as a result of this decision and the fact that they were two years apart, the two Howe boys had very little contact with each other except when twice a term their mother sent a cake. Geoffrey's son Alec eventually went to Marlborough; Colin's three sons to Winchester, one with a scholarship.

2

Manners Makyth Man

Ricardus Eduardus Gaufredus Howe – as Geoffrey was to
appear on the printed Long Roll of the school governing body,
masters, boys and quiristers (choristers) – arrived at Winchester in the autumn of 1940. He was thirteen years old and
the impact of this unique English institution on the sensitive,
gifted boy from South Wales with a non-conformist background was cataclysmic. Winchester provided the opportunity
to work and prove his academic ability in an atmosphere of
excellence, create lifelong friends, follow up a host of interests
and begin to develop a personal credo and passion for politics
and achievement which remains to this day.

Over London and the south-eastern counties, Spitfires fought
the Battle of Britain. In Winchester, the new boys – or men
in College parlance – joined a still privileged, if spartan, society
in which butlers waited at table, at least until war put an
end to all that, and a series of tradesmen would come in to
lay out their wares in the hall : – shoes one day, shirts, braces
and pullovers another. A barber would come once a week and
cut the young men's hair or sell them toothpaste and shaving
cream. In the town some shops bore the College arms together
with affirmation of their appointment to the Gentlemen Commoners of Winchester College. Nevertheless, ever implicit in
the privilege was the moral duty of the Wykehamist to help
those who were less fortunate, which is the underlying meaning

of the school motto 'Manners makyth man'.

Although on the Roll of Scholars as an exhibitioner, Geoffrey went into E house, known as Freddy's, not College, which was reserved for full Scholars. At that time there were seventy Scholars in College and about 400 Commoners in ten houses located nearby in the town. 'I was rather glad not to be in College because it was a forcing house,' he says today.

Winchester provided a highly communal existence with its own language and customs or notions, which, like the verdict on history of the book, *1066 and All That*, tended to be good, or bad. It was a bad notion for example to go up to books (the main school) to divs (classes) without a socius (companion). Scholars had their own uniform with black pin-striped trousers and black stuff gown. The Gentlemen Commoners wore grey flannels and rough tweed jackets during the week and, until the exigencies of war brought the custom to an end, morning dress and top hats on Sundays. Except for games they always wore strats (straw boaters with a house colour on the hat band). To break this rule was a punishable offence in the form of caning by one's elders and betters and the more powerful – in other words prefects. There were two forms of beating – the traditional flat approach by a senior prefect, and shavering in which the cane was flicked at a young bottom with a kind of slicing action.

'One was shavered literally every day for all sorts of trivial offences,' says Michael Nightingale of Cromarty, then known as Michael or Kim and one of Geoffrey's closer friends. He is now chairman of the Chillington Corporation plc and a board member of the Commonwealth Development Corporation. 'In the dormitory if you didn't clean your teeth or put your shoes straight or there was a pillow fight, a house prefect would come round and say: "All bend over". We were usually in pyjamas. Today it would appal people but being shavered didn't worry us at all. On the other hand, being beaten did actually hurt and left wheals for several days.' Fagging was an everyday duty for juniors with the younger boys described as 'men in sweat' as they fetched and carried for prefects a mere four years their senior.

Cold baths were another institution of those wartime days. Each boy would shed his pyjamas in the dormitory, wrap round a towel and run up to the bathroom, in which about six metal tubs were set out on a concrete floor, each filled with cold water. The first person often had to 'break the ice', since the tubs were usually filled last thing at night. In Geoffrey's time the taps were kept running as each man submerged himself up to the neck – a bit like a sheep dip – and then leapt out to the illusion of tingling heat and the reality of energy. While there was a rota for the occasional hot bath to follow sporting activity, it was the trauma of the cold bath which led a group of Geoffrey's friends, in particular Michael Nightingale, to form the Cold Bath Club when they left, meeting regularly and for some years writing round-robin foolscap letters, the last recipient adding his news at the bottom and chopping off his previous contribution before sending it on to the next member.

School society was totally gregarious and virtually the only respite and privacy was to be found in the Winchester equivalent of the study. Even here escape from the crowd was only partial. About thirty open-sided cubby-holes or toys, as they were called, were ranged round the main hall of Freddy's with a further ten in a room upstairs. Here the schoolboys kept their personal possessions and, since convention ruled against disturbing a man in his toys, it was possible to read, write a letter and even relax.

New men like Geoffrey were presented with a tege (pronounced T.J.), a protector who helped initiate them to notions good and bad and life in the public school generally; and Geoffrey found himself attached to Robert Sheaf, one year his senior, and destined, like Nightingale, to become a firm friend.

If the folklore of the ancient institution seemed almost regimental in its precision, the academic approach was designed for the encouragement of individual development and intellectual excellence and achievement. A new man would join one div or class with his immediate contemporaries for most subjects, such as English and religion, but be graded for others, including mathematics, according to ability. Effectively this meant the exceptional thirteen-year-old might be years ahead in one or more areas and make older friends as well as progress and yet still keep in regular contact with his peers. 'Your timetable was tailored to you as an individual,' Sheaf says today.

13

It certainly suited the rather shy, serious, studious and bright young boy from Wales with even then an omnivorous appetite for facts and learning. Geoffrey was lucky to have had contact with the great classicist, Cyril Robinson, known affectionately as The Bin. He was the sort of teacher who treated pupils as people and scattered seeds, and indeed the flowers of a whole culture, as he taught what in many schools would be little more than precise linguistics and literature. With many memorable classes held in the drawing room of his home, the boys might arrive at 9 am, start off with Latin or Greek, then listen to a classical 78 rpm gramophone record (there were neither stereos nor cassettes), study photographs of Italian sculpture and conclude with a session on Roman history. ('It wasn't like lessons in most schools,' says Michael Nightingale. 'It was just one long symphony of joy.')

The Bin, who had incidentally been Hugh Gaitskell's house master, so approved of the democratic practices of the ancient world that Geoffrey's form became a boule (Greek for legislative council) and themselves decided on details of their syllabus and timetable. It is noticeable today how often Sir Geoffrey invokes the same sort of principle with the people with whom he works, taking the chair but ensuring the more junior members of his team really can make a real contribution in terms of ideas and action. In addition, at school each member of the class had once a week to choose and learn by heart thirty lines of verse or prose to recite before his peers, which may have helped develop Geoffrey's extraordinary memory.

While Geoffrey was intensely interested in all things academic, as a teenager, apart from hill walking, he was not particularly fond of sports any more than he is today. However, each man was honour bound to do his more or less energetic duty in this sphere, notching up a specified number of hours or points for entry each week in a kind of house honesty book called the Ekka roll (ekka was Wykehamist shorthand for exercise, as mathma was for mathematics and pitch-up for parents). One game of football would rate so much in terms of time for the weekly personal record, squash or rowing on the river different scores. 'You could say play five games of squash and three games of fives or one of football,' says Sir Geoffrey today. 'But the most economical way of taking exercise in terms of time was to go for cross-country runs all of which were elaborately timed and about thirteen minutes equalled one half hour.'

However if sport was calculated according to strict economy of time and effort, the young Geoffrey was not at all the simple swot. Classics led him into the archaeological society and, together with Michael Nightingale, he would cycle to explore local ancient Britain, once finding a Roman coin which glinted in the sun on a newly-ploughed sod. Even at school he never appeared assertive but somehow achievement followed his involvement. He was a keen member of the photographic society and founded, with Nightingale, the film society. An ambitious project to film the school at work and play failed to win the approval of the headmaster, Spencer Leeson, who later became Bishop of Peterborough. However, they rented a regular diet of movies, often silent, for which he and Nightingale researched and chose suitably tense or romantic music leaving Geoffrey with highly catholic taste and an enjoyment, it could almost qualify as an addiction, for music while he works. In his study today, Sir Geoffrey will write speeches and plough through the papers in his ministerial boxes to the accompaniment of a mixture of opera, symphony or jazz.

At Winchester he was also secretary to the debating society and, in one early speech, took a traditionally conservative approach opposing the public ownership of the mines (the National Coal Board, now British Coal, only came into existence in 1947). It may seem an unlikely topic for keen debate in an English public school of the day but Winchester provided a goodly quota of left-wing intellectuals on the staff including Eric James, who organized the debating society, and produced some of the keener minds of the post-war Labour Party. Sir Stafford Cripps, Hugh Gaitskell and Richard Crossman were all Wykehamists, but before the young Geoffrey's time. Eric James, whom Sir Geoffrey remembers as 'a socialist and atheist and terrific', later became high master of Manchester Grammar School, a member of the House of Lords and vice-chancellor of York University.

Even then some of the threads of Sir Geoffrey's personal philosophy were beginning to emerge and some twenty years later he was to express concern about the impact of monopolistic

power on individual responsibility in the aftermath of the Aberfan disaster and Inquiry, at which he represented a number
of the local colliery workforce.

Equally prescient and more obviously radical was one of
his last appearances before his fellow men at Winchester in
favour of equal pay and opportunity for women. 'The Com-
moner Secretary (R.E.G. Howe (E)), proposing,' a subsequent
issue of *The Wykehamist* reported, 'tried to clear away the mass
of superstitious prejudices inherited by Wykehamists. Women
were supposed to be irrational and to make bad politicians,
bad doctors and bad lawyers. Their duty, so it was supposed,
was to relinquish their ambitions and inflict themselves on
men. These prejudices were worked into a large generalization
which, being a generalization, was false. Not every woman
was irrational or unstrung: only by the true acceptance of
able women could we get real democracy. By this acceptance
we should be completing the process of women's emancipation
from the complete captivity of primitive times, through the
now general toleration of some sort of participation to the final
consummation of equal pay. There was a general misconcep-
tion that this latter would lead to the dissolution of home life
and of the family. This was quite untrue. Howe concluded
by warning his audience against the sugar-coated missiles of
his opponents, who had all the jokes on their side, but none
of the arguments.'

One need scarcely say that the opposition feared for the
dissolution of the family, that marriage would become a losing
proposition and that the birth rate would decline. One College
speaker – J.A.Bolton – was thankful no woman was present
so that he could safely appeal to prejudice and ask the House
to forget reason. 'Who would be willing to pay women as much
for refereeing Sixes as a man?' *The Wykehamist* continues in
its report. 'The Motion said "every sphere of the national life".
Could we look forward with equanimity to the Court Circular
describing the Prime Minister and Mr Churchill's dinner at
Buckingham Palace, or to fashion plates of Mrs Proudie's attire
during her enthronement in Barchester Cathedral? Some
things like typing and manicuring – women could do . . . .' The
motion was defeated by 27 to 10. Little could the College
speaker have realized that his victory would be so hollow with

R.E.G.Howe continuing his mission some twenty years later by serving on a Conservative Party committee calling for a fair deal for the fair sex and that by 1975 that same R.E.G. Howe's wife Elspeth, by now Lady Howe, would become the first deputy chairman of the new-fangled Equal Opportunities Commission. Even more important, while the time still has to come for women to be ordained, let alone become bishops in the Church of England, its very real possibility now divides ecclesiastical circles. Meanwhile Court Circular reports about the Prime Minister and Mr Denis Thatcher have become unremarkable for their regularity.

By 1945 Geoffrey had become intensely involved in both religion and politics with Robert Sheaf his main partner for the sparring and exploring of ideas. He may have been playing chapel as a small boy but Sheaf remembers him as a marvellous listener. Religion played an important part in the closely-knit fabric of school life and one boy even invented his own faith, rigorously filling exercise books with the details of belief and worship. Atheism and agnosticism also attracted adherents among pupils as well as masters. So far as Geoffrey and Robert Sheaf were concerned, initially they became agnostic and deliberately refused to be confirmed at the appointed time. Robert Sheaf's father was a strong supporter of the Victorian T.H.Huxley's agnostic philosophy and undoubtedly influenced his son. While it was a stand of some independence against the norm, this lack of theological framework lasted only a short time. 'Geoffrey shattered me next time confirmation came round saying he was going to be confirmed,' Robert Sheaf recalls. 'I replied: "But Geoffrey we've agreed not to be." He then said something for which I am deeply grateful to him to this day. "I decided it's wrong to reject something before you've tried it." He's always been wise beyond his years. Most people don't think things through. He does and he did then.'

Following their confirmation, the two boys discovered and devoured books by C.S.Lewis and were then caught up in a peculiarly intense period of belief throughout the school, but particularly in E house, provoked by the mission to the school of Bishop Arthur Karney, Suffragan Bishop of Southampton. Following his visit, which voluntarily attracted increasing numbers to the daily services, small cells or groups were set up to discuss the meaning of the Bible and its relevance to their lives. In due course, several of Geoffrey's contemporaries went into the church.

Almost as part of this Christian zeal, the two boys also became passionately interested in politics. Indeed their political belief was intertwined with religion to the point that they discussed and formulated their own personal set of political philosophy and policies under the title of St Martha's Charter; St Martha being a beautiful small church on the Pilgrim's Way near the Sheaf home. The charter is no more but, heavily imbued with Christian doctrine about love in the sense of St Paul's 'caritas', it included such slogans as 'unity not uniformity' and a strong belief in the importance of individual freedom. It was a time when there was much talk about the need for direction of labour and their charter pronounced against state control, proclaiming instead an absolute conviction in the importance of the development of self and talents according to what the individual believed to be God's will – but always in the context of Christian concern and care. Naturally the two young men aimed high in their political fantasies. Robert Sheaf used to dream of running the Navy as Admiral of the Fleet. Geoffrey quite simply would run the Government. Certainly other friends thought he was prime ministerial material, too. 'There was no doubt he was determined to get on in the political world from a very early time,' Michael Nightingale says today. Even if St Martha's Charter has been lost, the need for self development combined with concern about others remains part of Sir Geoffrey's ethos more than forty years on. On a visit to his friend at Cambridge after the war, Robert Sheaf can remember Geoffrey pointing towards a leading light in the Labour club and saying that he would be truly amazed and incredulous to find the two Tories had just been discussing how to improve the condition of ordinary people in Britain. He also recalls a more recent comment on the Third World to the effect that those who think the process of development can be assisted simply by increasing financial aid to governments misunderstand the whole process of development.

Robert Sheaf has no doubts about the importance to him of their friendship: 'In a very unobtrusive way he just transformed my school days from something to be suffered and got through into a very good time.' A year older, he left school before Geoffrey and joined the Navy, flirted with the arts and read for the Bar in the same chambers as Geoffrey. He was converted to Roman Catholicism, fought Durham in the European elections in 1979 and finally became a permanent official in the Commission of the European Communities. Michael Nightingale has since been secretary of the Museums Association, a merchant banker, member of the General Synod of the Church of England, member of Kent County Council and mayor of Maidstone.

While Geoffrey was at Winchester, Britain was at war, a fact which increasingly influenced the behaviour of the young men as they drew near to leaving and the virtually automatic entry into the armed forces. At night they would often sleep in the improvised shelter and, as they grew older, watch for fires, an activity which involved tin hats and tea in the local ARP post. During this period Geoffrey discovered his unusually low requirement for sleep and was prepared to stand in for fellow men whose nature fought against such untimely duty. For him it was the beginning of an advantage given only to some chosen few, including Margaret Thatcher. To spend only four hours asleep, as Sir Geoffrey does normally during the week, frees time for reading which most people, even of similar intellectual ability, simply cannot find and which, over a lifetime, creates a fund of background knowledge which few can hope to match.

For a time Geoffrey ran Freddy's national savings campaign and won the inter-house competition. As a result, one master thought he could make a first-class election agent. Even The Bin was disappointed to find he was destined for the law, saying that he would make the kind of businessman Britain was likely to need in the post-war years. Geoffrey also organized the dig for victory and joined the officers cadet training unit. In this area he became so interested in making wirelesses or radios that he persuaded the house master to change the rules and allow men to have their own sets – provided they had been at Winchester two years and made them themselves. Sir Geoffrey jokes now that he was attracted to join the Signals when he attended a field day and saw members of this troop arrive by taxi while others marched out on foot. Meanwhile he had taken school certificate but not the equivalent of advanced level. His next step was to take the scholarship examinations to Oxford and Cambridge which required a wider syllabus. Because of Winchester's academic standing, Wykehamists were really in competition with each other rather than with boys from other schools. Towards the end of 1944 and the beginning of 1945, examinations became the norm as they sat papers from one cluster of colleges after another. In the third bout Geoffrey, by then a school prefect, won a minor scholarship to Trinity Hall Cambridge, to be taken up when he had completed his national service.

Although the end of the war in Europe was in sight, general expectation still reckoned on initial training in England followed by fighting in Burma or elsewhere in the Far East. His immediate destination however was a short course on physics and advanced mathematics at the University College of the South West in Exeter, to be followed later in the year by the full rigours of army life. By then the war against Japan had ended with the two terrible explosions of the atomic bomb, but national service continued.

3

Under Orders

In November 1986 nearly twenty men were checked by security as they arrived for a formal black-tie dinner at No 1, Carlton Gardens with the Secretary of State for Foreign and Commonwealth Affairs, Sir Geoffrey Howe. The guests included a fellow Tory Member of Parliament, a vicar, a doctor, a director of a major pharmaceutical company and several retired regular army officers. While such entertainment is an essential conversational and protocol ingredient of London's diplomatic minuet, there was an unusual sense of shared celebration on that particular evening. All were about sixty years old, all had been members of the same Officers Cadet Training Unit in Catterick, Yorkshire and passed out as second lieutenants exactly forty years before. Sir Geoffrey very much likes to keep in contact with old friends and the reunion was his idea. Out of the twenty-three men on the course in 1946, eighteen managed to be present.

Forty years back in time those same young men had just been transformed from raw national service recruits into junior officers of the Royal Signals. Geoffrey had enlisted as early as June 1944 but stayed on at Winchester to complete university entrance examinations, leaving at the end of the lent term to take advantage of the opportunity given by the regiment to attend a short course at Exeter. It was during this period that the Second World War came to an end and Britain rejected

21

Mr Winston Churchill as prime minister in favour of a reforming Labour administration.

However national, if not active, service continued and for Geoffrey, apart from the sight of dole queues in South Wales as a young boy, provided his first direct exposure to society at large, with a mixture of young men from very different backgrounds from all parts of the British Isles. And for all the community spirit of the war, the country was still conscious of class in a way which would now, in most areas of society, seem totally foreign – many barriers to opportunity, education, jobs and ownership having gradually been broken down. Even the monastic and hardening regime of Winchester can scarcely have prepared the academic, unphysical young man for the rigours of basic infantry training, the barracks and the parade ground at Aldershot, Hampshire and Wrotham, Kent. Wrotham in particular was quite horrifying with recruits racing everywhere and living in very primitive conditions including appalling sanitation. Known as 'the Monster' the sanitation was basically a large pipe with a series of holes cut into the top and serviced by occasional surges of water.

According to Ron Needs, administrative director of Beecham Pharmaceuticals who first met Geoffrey at Catterick: 'The challenge of officer cadet training at that time lay in the extraordinary contrasts. Out in the field exercises you were constantly under battle discipline. The cold, sheer discomfort and overwhelming pressure were designed to test the spirit as much as the body with tired minds stretched to solve the technical signals problems presented by instructors.'

The Officer Cadet Training Unit at Catterick was a complete transformation. Gone was the mud and filth in favour of absolute immaculate presentation of self and barracks. 'We spent hours and hours cleaning and hours and hours working and studying,' says Ron Needs. The course officer – Captain John Osborn, who has since been knighted and only retired as Tory MP for Hallam and Sheffield at the 1987 General Election – would inspect the room and equipment every morning including the shine on the beech strip floor. This the officer cadets would clean with wire wool and polish – unless they felt rich enough to pay an orderly to complete the tedious task. The same was true of boots, which had to be regularly maintained with spit and polish and more spit and polish with fingers in constant rotation to bring the leather to perfection. To overcome the sheer boredom of cleaning, the group would sit together talking as they polished, mainly about the war and army life. And if they did not appreciate it at the time, they later began to understand that the habit of cleanliness so well instilled could save men from sickness and equipment from breakdown in conditions of active service.

The course was highly technical, as well as practical and physical, and was spiced with simulated battle manoeuvres and general exposure to endurance up on the moors. The cadets had to learn the basics of electronics, design simple circuits, build small wireless sets and operate and maintain the heavy, relatively primitive radios then in military use. The war games were designed to test the reaction of potential officers under the stress of misadventure and the unexpected, as would be bound to happen in reality. The key messenger might fail to arrive because of an 'accident' and the officer trainees would simply have to accept the worst and do their best. On such exercises, men would carry equipment on their backs, do their own cooking (scarcely haute cuisine), share mess tins and slide at night into the discomfort of a bivouac tent for two.

The young soldiers' idea of an off-duty treat was to hitch a ride on a truck known as 'the passion wagon' to Richmond or Darlington, see a film and have a cheap tea in a local café or the Young Men's Christian Association. For the cadets an expression like 'passion wagon' was positively daring and altogether a joke. Sexual mores were very different and there was a singular dearth of young women for officer cadets to meet, let alone get to know.

What then of the man who became Second-Lieutenant Howe. According to Ron Needs: 'The technical challenge is something his mind could cope with quite readily. He had an immense capacity for work and as a leader too he was good. Where he was less comfortable was the sheer physical nature of these activities, so much jumping, running, leaping, charging, carrying, doing physical things; none of which really suited his temperament or character. I was always amazed when he told me he had climbed the local mountain on an expedition in Kenya. But of course he was inclined to seize

23

opportunities and do things. If we were out somewhere and there was something interesting to go to visit such as local ruins or a beauty spot, he was always very happy to detach himself from army life and go and do something civilized.' As Foreign Secretary Sir Geoffrey still has this habit and, given the chance, even on official visits, will switch off and explore.

In fact, Ron Needs perhaps should not have been quite so surprised that his friend should have undertaken the challenge of Mount Kenya. His home at Port Talbot backed onto a steep hill; he had run, cycled and developed a passion for hill walking at Winchester and at Catterick continued his enjoyment of the hills. He spent at least one weekend away with a small party including fellow trainee officer cadet Martin Bott, climbing Cross Fell and walking between twenty-five and thirty miles in the day. Geoffrey also created a reputation in boxing, not for prowess or agility – although he was slim as a young man – but for sheer courage and guts as he rose repeatedly to his feet for more battering punishment.

Second-Lieutenant Needs finished the course as batonniere, Geoffrey came second. It was Captain Osborn's first course and he remembers the group for its outstanding spirit. There was even the day when, not having ridden a motor cycle for about a year, he had to lead a trek up hill, down dale and through streams, in the first of which he got stuck. The course cadets navigated the mud, rode up the next hill, parked their vehicles, came to the rescue, put their officer back in front and meekly set off when he once again gave the command: 'Follow me'. 'I was conscious of those two (Needs and Howe) and probably one more,' says Sir John today. 'But I never thought I had a Foreign Secretary and Chancellor of the Exchequer in the course. And I never thought I would be an MP myself.' As it happened, Sir John went into the steel industry and, because of the political traumas with nationalization followed by denationalization, found himself drawn into battle with the Socialists, became a local Conservative candidate and in due course MP. In 1962 a young lawyer came up to him at the Conservative Party conference at Llandudno and said: 'Hello, Sir. How are you, Sir?' It was Geoffrey Howe, by then at the bar and keenly involved in the Bow Group. Sir John says it was only ten years before their roles were reversed and it was he who had to call Geoffrey, Sir, by then also an MP, on his appointment as Solicitor-General.

Ron Needs finished his national service in the Middle East and happened to catch up with his fellow Signals officer in the early days of the Bow Group, when Fred Tuckman, now MEP for Leicester, persuaded him to go to a meeting addressed by Vic Feather, General Secretary of the Trades Union Congress and later to become a member of the House of Lords. Geoffrey was in the chair. 'I had no idea of his passion for politics until that moment,' says Needs.

Martin Bott, who has since become Professor of Geophysics at Durham University, a Fellow of the Royal Society and was partly responsible for finding sedimentary basins in the Irish Sea and near West Shetland, simply thought he was a very able person, who got on well with almost everyone, and would do well in his chosen profession of the law. After passing out at Catterick, he and Geoffrey went out by ship to Nairobi to join the East Africa Command. He went south to Tanganyika, Geoffrey north to Nanyuk under Mount Kenya, which they climbed together aided and abetted by mules. Kilimanjaro Howe tackled on his own, a trip which lasted some five days and cost £8 complete with four porters and a guide. He described this particular adventure in graphic terms on the radio programme, *Man of Action*, which was broadcast by the BBC on the Third Programme in 1977, when he was shadow Chancellor of the Exchequer and increasingly in the public eye.

'I still remember the struggle up the last 3,000 feet of scree and snow on Kilimanjaro, stopping very frequently in response to the African guide's gentle invitation – (phonetically) "Nataka chai kidogo, Bwana?" – for a drink of cold sweet tea,' he told radio listeners. 'I remember too that almost as soon as I reached the top of Africa's highest mountain, with its breathtaking view into the volcanic crater and out over the plains of Tanganyika, I fell fast asleep and stayed asleep for two hours.' Such activity combined with a need for the restorative powers of sleep are difficult now to imagine in a man who is distinctly portly and is renowned for his ability to retire at 2 am and rise at 6 am.

However spiritually uplifting the sense of space and physical achievement involved in communing with these two major mountains, the period in East Africa, with its close contacts with the indigenous soldiers, proved even more important in the development of the future Foreign Secretary's personal and political philosophy. While there were a number of other English officers, the unit consisted of black troops, not all English-speaking. Duties extended beyond communications between the three battalions of the northern area into current affairs for the soldiers, generally focused on pamphlets produced by the Labour Government thousands of miles away in London. Howe found himself in Swahili trying to explain the *raison d'etre* of Empire and British control, the theory of common citizenship and the reason why Bwana King George VI was better than Bwana Stalin.

Pressure for independence was beginning to emerge with one particularly early bloody warning of future atrocities and terrorism. At Christmas 1947, precursors of Mau-Mau rampaged through the local reserve with obscene mutilation of their victims. For all the horror, the young Welsh officer had a relaxed view of life, so much so that on reaching for the telephone in the headquarters mess and hearing a voice say: 'This is the brigade area commander', his immediate reply was: 'Oh, this is Father Christmas.' But he returned home to be demobbed in the summer of 1948 convinced, as he had been at Winchester, of the right of each man, black as well as white, to choose for himself and the importance of Africa.

4

Salad Days

A former army officer and twenty-one years old, Geoffrey Howe arrived at Trinity Hall, Cambridge as an exhibitioner to read law and step onto the first rung of his political career. Life under a Labour government in post-war Britain, combined with direct experience of Labour control at home in South Wales and his fundamental faith in the rights and importance of the individual as against those of the state, had convinced him that this was the right road for him and for the country. It was an important decision. While the seeds of political theory and service had been sewn at home and cultivated at Winchester, the family tradition had until then been Liberal. The words of the old Welsh drinking song 'Lloyd George knew my father, Father knew Lloyd George' were, and are, actually true when sung by the Howe sons. And young Howe had even canvassed for a Liberal candidate in the 1945 election soon after he left school. However he now believed that the post-war Conservative Party could and should inherit the mantle of liberalism, which for him implied beliefs in free market economics and concern for humanity.

The Cambridge he entered in 1948 was very different from today when undergraduates usually arrive straight and fresh from school armed with their relevant quota of advanced grades but very little experience of any other work or world. In those post-war years, such youthfulness was uncommon, except among the limited numbers of young women of sufficient intellectual achievement to pass the testing entrance examination hurdles into the two female colleges of Newnham and Girton. Single sex colleges were the historic norm, ignorance of the other sex widespread. As well as the new male intake of young men, who like Howe had completed national service, others had actually fought in the war and in some cases were rounding off a university career rudely interrupted by its outbreak. Such students did have money to spend but for others grants were few and the lifestyle for the majority, mainly middle class and public school, was comfortable but certainly not opulent. Cyprus sherry at about 7s 6d a bottle was the cheapest party drink, men friends might be invited to dinner, girls taken decorously to tea dances as well as the more formal long dress occasions in the Dorothy Café.

One of the oldest colleges, Trinity Hall was small, traditionally connected with the law and suited the young man from Wales who soon found himself sharing rooms with Gordon Adam, also reading law. Adam came from Ulster but had spent fifteen of his early years in Canada and, like Howe, looked on England somewhat as an outsider. The accommodation was spacious, spartan and extremely cold with, in that first winter, slate being sold as a heatless substitute for coal. By their second year Adam arranged for sacks of peat to be sent from Northern Ireland.

Politically this was a very exciting time in the Cambridge University Conservative Association (CUCA). The new blood fed its enthusiasm for fighting Socialism with meetings and debates and membership soared to about 1,200 out of a total undergraduate population of about 7,000. Certainly politics became Howe's main outside interest as he participated in both the union and CUCA. Then as now the union was the debating society of Cambridge, not only on political subjects. The president, traditionally elected for one term, would take the chair, with guests well-known in their fields invited to speak for and against the motion, supported in turn by leading students. And for the main participants it was still a black-tie evening. Howe would contribute to political debates and is remembered for a very studied uncharismatic style, which may explain why, although he became an officer of the union, unlike contemporaries who also joined him in the House of Commons, he never won the presidential accolade. If Welsh passion there was, he kept it well hidden.

In CUCA he was more successful, taking over the top role in the second term of his final year and was immediately followed by Richard (Dick) Stone with whom he was then sharing rooms. Stone was another student studying law whose background did not fit the conventional English mould in that he had been evacuated to Canada for part of the war. All three were good friends. Richard Stone was later to be best man when Geoffrey married Elspeth Shand; Geoffrey was best man at the weddings of both Stone and Adam; they are godfathers to two of the Howe children; and one of Geoffrey's seven godchildren is an Adam.

While Richard Stone and Geoffrey Howe were the more politically active, Gordon Adam, who later became a general manager and director of Barclays, was closely involved in efforts on the street hustings on behalf of the local Tory candidate in the 1950 General Election. Dressed in an old mackintosh and cloth cap and sucking a pipe, he acted as unofficial but premeditated heckler shouting from the back of any crowd: 'What are you going to do for the poor?' At this point, Howe would reply to the downbeat stranger: 'That's a very good question, Sir' and take the opportunity to expand on the manifesto.

Meetings were much livelier then and a genuine, if somewhat specialized, attraction. Without television to dull the appetite with a surfeit of political ideas and debate, as well as provide comfortable entertainment beside the fire, CUCA gatherings gave students an opportunity for face-to-face encounter with the more and the less famous. As officers they would entertain the guest, perhaps even make a good impression and, if they were really lucky, begin an acquaintance which could lead to political patronage. Active membership of CUCA was one of the traditional stepping stones to a parliamentary career and Members of Parliament were very willing to leave London for East Anglia to address an audience of perhaps as many as 150 keen young minds. But unlike some CUCA chairmen, Geoffrey Howe did not leave Cambridge with a clutch of political sponsors who would encourage him in the Conservative

Party at large and even possibly put in a good word with the local hierarchy when the opportunity came for a seat.

In his Cambridge days, Denzil Freeth and Norman St John-Stevas, both ex-presidents of the union, were the names people would frequently mention in attempts to spot the political high fliers. Even then the overt catholicism and delight in pure debating gamesmanship of St John-Stevas injected some caution into predictions that he might rise to the top of the Tory Party and become prime minister. Both, of course, did go into Parliament. St John-Stevas, who went on to Oxford and Yale, rose as high as Leader of the Commons and Arts Minister in the Thatcher Government. When the Prime Minister no longer retained him as one of her ministerial team, he found he had a new career as chairman of the Royal Fine Art Commission and, after the 1987 General Election, membership of the House of Lords. Denzil Freeth resigned and went into the City.

When Stone, now a QC and a Wreck Commissioner, attended a college reunion in the mid-1980s, an elderly tutor asked whether he had ever thought his friend Geoffrey Howe would go so far. Stone admitted he too had not expected such political success. But he also remembered introducing Geoffrey to his adopted Canadian wartime uncle, a shrewd Toronto businessman, just after leaving university, who said Howe was the best informed and expressed person of any age group he had met on his visit to Britain.

The future of the British lands in Africa was a major issue at the time and CUCA members were sufficiently fired by a speech by Lord Swinton to form a special group for black students with Conservative sympathies from that continent. For some it took courage to belong, since they could all too easily be hauled up when they returned home for daring to step out of line. Geoffrey Howe was very committed to early advance for the colonies and he and Richard Stone, whose father had been the last English Chief Justice of Bombay, would argue the advantages and disadvantages of British withdrawal well into the night. He also carried one university debate on the subject, when the more cautious were advocating a policy of much longer-term delay to independence.

Howe had already learnt the virtues of professionalism

including proper briefing and preparation before performance. Together with Richard Stone and another friend from Clare College, Jimmy Davis, who also later became a barrister, he travelled north to help a local doctor who was campaigning as Tory candidate in the unwinnable seat at Crewe. One evening all three were to speak at Nantwich with the exciting (for students) possibility, since the candidate was absent, that their views and persona might hit the local press and they would enjoy a first real taste of fame. All three spoke and next day they bought the newspaper to read the headline: 'Young Tory lashes red juveniles' over a sizeable chunk of space recording Geoffrey Howe's comments on the latest Fabian pamphlet. At the bottom it simply said that two other young Conservatives also spoke. Stone and Davis were very put out. 'There's a lesson in that,' says Stone today. 'We were just handing out the usual hack party line. Geoffrey read something from the other side, analysed it and gave a convincing answer, if not in fact complete demolition of the argument. But it nearly broke up the speaking tour.' By the 1955 election Geoffrey Howe was fighting the Labour-held seat on his own home ground in South Wales and Stone was helping his campaign.

The three young men would travel in a 1936 Standard 10 bought by Stone in 1950 and which had been laid up during the war. Affectionately known as Blossom, she provided the backcloth for happy picnics en route when the three would munch sandwiches and talk about the meaning of life. She also brought them within glimpse of an untimely end when her brakes failed on a Pennine hill but the wheels held the corner at the bottom.

Soon after leaving Cambridge, Richard Stone was present on another occasion when disaster all but struck. By then Geoffrey Howe had met and married Elspeth and they had been on a sailing holiday to France with a group of friends. On the way back from Normandy in the chartered ketch *Kirsty* they hit heavy weather, lost the dinghy, tore their sails and began to ship water. Stone remembers Elspeth Howe passing buckets up from the bilges until they finally anchored in the bay off Seaford, Sussex. But their troubles had yet to end. Next morning the ratchet broke on the manual winch as they were winding up the anchor, snapping back to leave first one man, then a second, then a third unable to help as their hands took the blow. They could do nothing but fly the Red Ensign upside down and hope someone would notice their distress signal. It was spotted from the beach and in due course the lifeboat towed the boat into Newhaven where the three men caught a bus to hospital in Brighton for treatment for the broken bones in their hands. Many years later, when speaking at Swansea, Howe was to discover from the owner's widow that the *Kirsty* had eventually gone down at sea with loss of life.

Of course Cambridge was not all politics or law for Geoffrey Howe, although he was much more interested in politics than women. But even CUCA had its lighter side, staging what it liked to think was the dance of the year in the Dorothy Café with white tie and advertising, 'dancing to four bands on three floors'. In any event it was sufficiently notable in the social calendar for Howe's brother Colin, by then at Oxford, to organize a coach full of friends to visit the rival university for the occasion. Howe returned the compliment by writing a regular weekly column for Oxford's *Isis* including some theatre criticism. Geoffrey had a girlfriend in the Footlights, which was in sparkling form, this being the era of musical productions by Julian Slade, who went on to write the ever-green *Salad Days*. He also renewed his friendship with Ruth Jenkins, whom he had seen on a joint family holiday in Scotland and who had a local catering job. While the parents on both sides nursed hopes that the two members of the younger generation would marry, they were at a stage when both wanted to develop a wider circle of friends. Geoffrey rowed a little and maintained his interest in climbing, even to the point of keeping a rope in his college rooms. His parents would occasionally stay at one of the grander hotels; his father, to whom Geoffrey now bears an almost uncanny resemblance, very Welsh and very proud of the son who was making good. The son perhaps enjoyed his time at university more than his tutor, also a Wykehamist, might have wished and he left Cambridge with an upper second in law, not the first-class honour degree for which a more single-minded scholar might have hoped.

5

Taking a Bow

Geoffrey Howe's dual interest in law and politics flowed naturally into his new life in London after graduation in the summer of 1951. He went into chambers in the Middle Temple, became the pupil of Norman Richards QC, later the Official Referee, and was called to the Bar in 1952. He shared a Hampstead flat with fellow barrister Patrick Jenkin, who also entered Parliament and became Secretary of State for Social Services, Industry and the Environment before removal from the Thatcher Government. He is now a member of the House of Lords.

On the political front Geoffrey Howe found a natural home and métier in the newly-founded Bow Group, which had just been created by a small group of former leaders of university conservative associations. As often happens, the origins of an extremely influential organization were somewhat haphazard. Every year keen Tory undergraduates assemble for a jolly gathering run by the Federation of University Conservative and Unionist Associations (FUCUA). In March 1950 the chairman, Bruce Griffiths, who was to become a QC and then circuit judge, proposed and Peter Emery, now Sir Peter and Tory MP for Honiton, seconded a motion to create a centre for new graduates to meet and continue their active interest in Conservative politics and policies.

'We needed to harness the intellectual abilities of those who had had a good time in Conservative right-wing politics in universities,' explains Judge Griffiths today. 'The YCs (Young Conservatives) were not attractive, nor were constituency associations, and the Coningsby Club and the United and Cecil Club were both dining clubs. There was lacking in the Conservative Party an intellectual base such as the Fabian Society provided.' At that time, Tory thinking tended to emanate under the auspices of the Conservative Political Centre, which produced pamphlets from within the party headquarters. The new organization, while declared to be wholly and loyally Conservative in outlook, was to retain absolute independence of Central Office.

Bruce Griffiths and Peter Emery met with others in Denzil Freeth's flat in Battersea to discuss the next steps and found support from Colonel Joel, then an influential London politician, who arranged for them to have accommodation in the Bromley by Bow Conservative Club in London's East End. The group was set up there in February 1951 and held its first annual dinner, at which Sir Edward Boyle was speaker, at the Bow Bells pub. The first pamphlet, *Coloured Peoples in Britain*, published in 1952, price 6d, tackled a virtually new problem in British politics to such effect that No 10 Downing Street asked for a number of copies.

Griffiths first met Geoffrey Howe over coffee when spending a weekend at Cambridge as chairman of FUCUA. They found they both came from South Wales, had similar interests in law and politics and became firm friends. Judge Griffiths describes the Bow Group founders as enthusiastic but perhaps somewhat flamboyant, and is doubtful whether they would have ever had the commitment to make the new organization become a permanent as well as provocative part of the political scene. 'So many things fade within two years unless you have someone to take over in the second and third,' he says now. 'I am sure the thing would have died but for Geoffrey and some others like him – for example James Lemkin – who were good solid chaps. They really took it over. Geoffrey in particular had a more penetrating attitude to see what potentials there were for the future. The amount of work he put into it, getting it onto a firm, sensible business-like basis was very considerable and a very substantial achievement.'

James Lemkin, an Oxford man who is now senior partner in a major firm of London solicitors, became the second chairman. He was succeeded by Dick Stone, one of Geoffrey's Cambridge friends and by then also at the Bar; Sir Robin Williams, also Cambridge, an insurance broker, followed on and in 1955 Howe took over; a year in which he also first tested his metal as a parliamentary candidate in the Labour-dominated Welsh seat of Aberavon. The roll-call of Bow Group chairmen since those days reflects the precarious nature of politics; with people like David Howell and Leon Brittan QC, whose careers have waxed and waned (at least temporarily); Julian Critchley who remains firmly independent on the backbenches and Christopher Brocklebank-Fowler who, as Tory MP for Norfolk North West, opted for the Social Democratic Party mid-Parliament in 1981 and was defeated in 1983; and again others like John MacGregor and Norman Lamont, who are still climbing the political ladders of their careers, their respective jobs in 1988 being Minister for Agriculture and Financial Secretary to the Treasury.

In the early 1950s full Bow Group membership was open to men and women under thirty-six and of Conservative views at a cost of 10s 6d, with a 5s country membership for those who did not live or work within fifteen miles of Hyde Park Corner. It aimed to create a rallying point in London and large provincial cities for people who had become interested in politics at university and others keen to undertake political research in congenial and effective company. Speakers were invited to address off-the-record meetings, which soon moved from the East End into respected institutions in central London such as the Constitutional Club in Northumberland Avenue and later the Caxton Hall. However, the research groups formed the crucial essence of the operation and its subsequent network of friends. Whatever the subject, small groups of members would try to push aside personal prejudice and past practice and aim at objectivity in both their research and conclusions. Reports were meant to be factual, well-balanced and provocative and had, before publication, to win the support of the Bow Group as a whole. An open meeting would be held, the report presented and a vote taken on the quality of the research and ideas, not the policies proposed, since the group had and has no collective policy.

For Geoffrey Howe, raised in the rigorous analytical and intellectual climate of Winchester, the Bow Group provided a useful political scene for a wide-ranging investigation of Tory philosophy, policies and ideas. He became a prolific pamphleteer, his first publication emerging in 1954 when he was treasurer. Called *The Life-blood of Liberty – Some Proposals for Local Government Reform*, it was the group's fourth pamphlet and cost 1s. His collaborators included his wife Elspeth, Anthony Buck, Beryl Cooper, Colin Jones, James Lemkin, Antony Lines and Robert Sheaf, a Winchester friend.

The pamphlet still makes relevant reading today. How, it asked, could local councils be called democratic when less than half the electorate troubled to vote and they represented the community with such casual inaccuracy. But the strength of democracy should not be measured in narrow mathematical terms and local government did provide a valuable element in society. 'There are at least two reasons,' the introduction continued, 'why no one can afford to ignore its present and future condition. First, we must remember the role of local authorities as powerful institutions apart from the state itself. They should be regarded as bastions against a threat of centralised tyranny in this country. They have an essential part to play in preserving the balance of a democratic society.

'Secondly, we should respect and value the elected composition of all the local councils. They are an invaluable training ground in the principles of democracy and an excellent means of spreading and strengthening those principles deep in the foundations of the state. There is today widespread controversy about the condition of local government. On the one hand, the system is stated to be in irreparable decay; on the other, it is said to be as virile and effective as ever ...'

A pithy commentary but somewhat unsettling today when a Tory government has found the state so threatened by some of those self-same bastions, particularly in Labour-controlled inner urban areas, and enlarged of course by subsequent reform, that it has abolished the Greater London Council and the English metropolitan counties in the struggle for power. It has also set up urban development corporations outside democratic control and introduced proposals, where people so wish, for breaking down the municipal control of housing estates and transferring the control of schools to parents.

The pamphlet's conclusions were unusually flexible and tried to take account of places as they were rather than to fit some bureaucratic vision. 'Local institutions should be shaped by the social and geographical structure of the peoples and the places which they serve. Local authorities are more than mere administrative machines. They cannot operate without reference to the loyalties of their citizens or to the realities of local geography. Reformers should recognize that the inhabitants of a village or small town may only feel real loyalty to that small unit, however much the theorists would prefer them to be devoted to the five-year plan of a regional board. Reform should not regard uniformity as an important object. The pattern of our towns and countryside is anything but uniform: some villages have scarcely changed in centuries, and ancient loyalty to the parish remains more lively than any other. In our large cities on the other hand, and still more in the sprawling industrial areas, the strongest local loyalty is probably to the football team, and most families know nothing of those who live in the next street. Any structure of local government must recognize such differences in the scale of loyalty and in the pattern of society.'

Geoffrey Howe then made suggestions for two-tier authorities in the big cities, with planning, engineering and technical services the responsibility of the top tier. The lower tier would concentrate locally on all the human social services. Even in 1954 he and his team understood the potential power struggle which could arise between Whitehall and a Greater London Council. 'The idea of one major authority for the whole extent of Greater London has many disadvantages,' Howe wrote. 'The foremost is a constitutional one. Such a council would govern the affairs of about a quarter of the people of England and Wales. It would be a more revolutionary creation than a Welsh or Scottish Parliament. It is not impossible to foresee a major conflict arising between this body and the Queen's government itself. Moreover, a council of this sort, even with its second-tier authorities, would scarcely be a creature of local government as we conceive it. It might become more remote and inhuman than any previous organ of so-called local administration.'

The Greater London Council was set up in 1964. Under the leadership of Ken Livingstone, who has since become Labour MP for Brent East, the predicted struggle for power took place and the GLC was abolished in 1986.

Since London now has a void instead of a voice, the Bow Group alternative may be worth placing back in the ring. Howe divided London into six sectors, each with their own councils which would then nominate representatives to a special joint authority. This would have limited powers over broad matters of policy including the police, planning and major housing and development schemes. 'It would not be wise to leave final decisions in the few matters which affected the area as a whole to direct negotiations between these six councils,' he added. (The same might be said now of the thirty-two boroughs and the City Corporation.) A lower tier was proposed for local services.

So far as the rest of the country was concerned, the Howe pamphlet preached a doctrine of diversity. The package included: thirteen one-tier new counties focused on major cities such as Bristol, Hull, Coventry and Bournemouth and Poole; a number of new county boroughs; two-tier new counties for more rural areas; and parish councils in the countryside but not in towns, where it would be wishful to think they could impose a new and friendly feeling of neighbourhood. 'Even in a single street the inhabitants have little in common,' Howe writes. 'The father of each household probably goes one way to his work, and another for his beer; his football club lies somewhere else, and his chapel in a fourth direction (a little Welsh input there). Mother's interests are equally scattered: she shops in the town centre, and attends the Women's Institute in a different district. Children, too, live their lives in many places and with many different sets of people. If town dwellers are to be encouraged to take a more active part in governing their own local affairs, this must be done through the existing organs of community life. Many of these are probably undemocratic in an electoral sense. But democracy as a technical term is not a talisman of virtue. We can best build up democratic institutions in the towns, not by the imposition of the ballot box, but by the encouragement of active participation in the many voluntary bodies which already exist –

Parents' Associations for the schools, Leagues of Friends for the hospitals, Youth Organizations and Parish Societies. The scope for urban community life is there in abundance. There is no need to create an arid electoral framework to this end.'

A second Howe pamphlet was written with Colin Jones, for many years editor of *The Banker*. It emerged in July 1956 and was called *Houses to Let – the Future of Rent Control*. It cost 2s 6d and was published by the Conservative Political Centre, which had by now made overtures and its expertise available to the new, if still sturdily independent, group. So many Bow Groupers had contributed to the research and discussion that only one was mentioned: Jimmy Davis, who had again been a close Howe friend at Cambridge. It was a workmanlike document on a complex subject, which sears the emotions in terms of individual tragedies and homelessness but bores all but the experts when it comes to the details of law and finance. However Geoffrey Howe's faith in the market shines through. 'A scheme of control that stabilises rents below their ordinary market level is tantamount, in its effect, to a tax on landlords and a subsidy for their tenants,' begins the chapter on the price of control. 'It serves, in other words, as a compulsory redistributor of incomes. But there should be some logic ordering the incidence of the tax and the allocation of the subsidy.' It continues: 'The recipients of the subsidies are selected haphazardly with no conscious regard for their relative needs and quite regardless moreover of whether their landlords are wealthy or poor. Furthermore, the growing burden of this tax, and other consequences of the present system of control, have served to limit the supply of rentable accommodation; the indiscriminate distribution of the subsidy has helped to inflate the demand for housing; and both have contributed to further distortions in the economy at large.'

In later sections, the authors write: 'We believe that, in economic terms, the operation of the free market is likely to be the most purely efficient . . . Some provision should be made, if possible, to allow for the local retention or reintroduction of rent control in times and places of acute scarcity; and that some permanent provision should be made for the extended operation of notices to quit. Apart from these two features, the whole of the remaining structure of rent control in this country should be eliminated ... Is it wise, it may be asked, to introduce a measure which is likely to stimulate further wage claims, when we are struggling to find stability on the "plateau" of Mr Macmillan's dream? Of course, the present is always an unpopular time for doing anything which will raise prices; and any increase in prices can – and will – be used in support of wage demands. But such demands will not be avoided simply by seeking to deprive union leaders of every plausible argument in favour of their case. One can, on the other hand, prevent wage demands from leading to any substantial increase in wages by creating the conditions in which it is unlikely for unfounded wage claims to be conceded. In the creation of such disinflationary conditions the removal of rent control would serve a positively healthy purpose, by absorbing in the purchase of a necessity (accommodation) that spending power which would otherwise have an inflationary effect in other sectors of the economy ... Rent control, born of emergency and nurtured with some regard for principle, has now assumed the rigidity of age. Forty years on, it conforms to no consistent principles – economic, social or moral. It betokens wastage of housing, distortion in the economy – and injustice for many.' The then Housing Minister, Henry Brooke, decided such an approach was politically far too adventurous and the pamphlet has remained too radical for governments to this day.

In September 1959, Geoffrey Howe's name again featured on the masthead of another Bow Group pamphlet, this time with Tom Hooson, who later became Tory MP for Brecon and died in 1985. Howe was at that time once again Conservative candidate in his home constituency of Aberavon, South Wales. For this publication, the authors had a strong research team which included Ruth Gass, Bruce Griffiths, David Howell, Jeremy Lever, Russell Lewis and Sir Robin Williams. Without undue modesty, the introductory chapter, a call for courage, declared: 'Since the war, no political party has published a thorough analysis of the economic problems of Wales. Work for Wales has attempted this task.' A willing task it was because Howe was passionately fond of his homeland.

Again Geoffrey Howe's longer-term views and general philosophy about the role of the State stand the test of time. For example, 'any nationalistic attempt to achieve economic autarchy for Wales is anachronistic in a Europe which is rightly striving to liberalise trade within common markets and free trade areas.' Economic aid should be used only to prime the pump. 'The distinctive Tory contribution to Welsh politics should be to oppose the subsidy mentality and to work for a virile, flexible and thoroughly competitive Welsh economy. We should therefore oppose subsidies which are other than transitional for inefficient farms, marginal coal mines and declining industries. With economic assistance of this invigorating kind we should also be able to achieve an objective beyond that of maintaining employment: fostering a busier Wales with an expanding economy, a quicker circulation of money and a greater abundance of goods. It implies looking beyond the first priority of creating work for the unemployed. It means, for example, making jobs available to women who want to work. It means ensuring greater productivity in factory and farm. And it means encouraging tourism, despite its seasonal nature, because this brings money into Wales. Increased expenditure by tourists will increase employment in the distribution and service trades and ultimately the whole economy, for prosperity breeds prosperity.'

Further on the authors suggest that one stimulus would be a healthy dose of self-help, such as the creation of small Welsh companies backed by local finance and an expansion of investment facilities. 'If no one else embarks upon the enterprise, could the Development Corporation for Wales create a Welsh Unit Trust, with investments in public companies with interests in Wales? Could not Wales become a test area for the Industrial Investment Certificates recently advocated? (In a CPC publication called *Everyman a Capitalist*). These would be a form of Unit Trust Certificate, with certain tax advantages and as easily purchased as National Savings Certificates ... Governments can only give leadership: the greater role should be played by the initiative of the Welsh people.'

Other proposals included an injection of private money into the marketing of coal. 'The Coal Board's massive marketing structure should be broken into independent, smaller units. The drab terminology of Coal Utilisation Councils and Fuel

Efficiency Services should give way to Fireside Centres and Clean Coal Bureaus.'

They pointed out that development areas tended to feel the worst effects of recessions and, although diversification had reduced the problem's scale, it could not be solved by this means alone unless Britain could afford to disregard economic factors in defiance of the forces of international competition. 'It is impossible to go so far,' the authors wrote. 'But the community should continue to devote a margin of its resources to the maintenance of full employment in the more vulnerable parts of the country. Clear limits must be set to the extent of intervention: the cost and period should, whenever possible, be directly ascertainable and under constant parliamentary review and justification; resources should not be devoted to the preservation of industries or communities which can never be economically viable; and resources should not be diverted to this purpose to such an extent as to threaten Britain's competitive efficiency. By the same standard intervention is justifiable for the purpose of cushioning the impact of inevitable economic change, as well as caring for those who cannot alter the pattern of their lives sufficiently to adapt themselves to the change.'

The views of the future Chancellor of the Exchequer were already well established, although it is perhaps surprising that he did not follow up one point in their proposed ten-year programme which was of particular relevance to areas with high unemployment. 'People must be given incentives to move from declining communities to places with better prospects of work,' it says. 'Adequate compensation for redundancy must be assured. Mortgages to cover legal and removal expenses, as well as the cost of buying a new house, should be made available. A redundant worker should be allowed to set off any loss incurred in selling his old house against his future tax liability.'

Howe's next publication under Bow Group auspices was a contribution to *Principles in Practice*, a series of Bow Group essays for the 1960s, which covered such policy areas as education, defence, foreign affairs, the Commonwealth, leisure and overseas development. A number of Bow Group members were involved, including Tim Raison, then working on the *New Scientist*; David Howell, also at that time a journalist following a period in the Treasury; James Lemkin, solicitor and three times chairman of the group; Russell Lewis, an economist, then working for the European Economic Community; Godfrey Hodgson, then with *The Observer* and a Canadian Len Beaton, then defence and air correspondent of *The Guardian*. (Raison and Howell later became Tory MPs and ministers but then returned to the backbenches; Lewis, after running the Conservative Political Centre for a time, has become a journalist; Hodgson combines books with journalism; Beaton died when he was director of the Institute of Strategic Studies.)

Howe's subject was the role of the social services. Once again his writing called for much more self reliance and a retreat of State responsibility to those areas which people cannot manage on their own. It has taken a long time for the views he was then airing to gain much credence in the party, let alone the country at large. To start with his conclusion: 'A deliberate move must therefore be made towards the creation of a "self-help" State in which the individual is more and more encouraged to provide for himself and his family. Conservatives who have proclaimed their objectives in this way have too often been busy sliding, if not marching, in the opposite direction. Britain's social policy has been dominated for too long by attitudes that were fashioned in the Webb–Beveridge era. If resources are to be found for the remodelling of our cities and the recreation of our social capital on a scale that is appropriate to our national wealth and if taxes are to be kept at a tolerable level, radical reform of the social services is overdue. Here is a challenge to fresh Conservative thinking and vigorous Conservative government for the next twenty-five years.'

It is indeed, as has become obvious in the struggles for more resources within the health service and education. All the time however Howe set a context of continuing care. Conservatives were, or should be, he said, quickly roused to anger or compassion by poverty or hardship which struck them as intolerable in a civilized society. 'They should be as readily moved as any Socialist to look for reserves of wealth which can legitimately be tapped to abate the evil. But their approach should be pragmatic rather than emotional. Not "How can we tolerate such wealth?" but "Where can we raise the money?" '

And again: 'There is no justification for taking tax from some to meet needs of others which they can meet themselves. Our tax structure should be as non-progressive as possible. And equality should never feature as an object of our social policy.' And later: 'Few Conservatives would doubt that the social services for the most part are here to stay. But we should hesitate to agree with Sir Keith Joseph who, while seeking "scope for sensible men to provide additional protection or amenity for their families and themselves on top of the State provision" plainly expects the State to go on making the basic provision for all of us for ever ... Even Enoch Powell seems to have accepted the inevitability of gradualism ... This is a long way from the doctrine on which Conservatives of my generation were nurtured. "Our civilisation", we were told, "is built up on private property." It was our objective to "restore the freedom of each individual to spend his income as he thinks best or to save it in order to create more wealth or to provide for some future emergency". Has all this been swept away?' He quotes with approval Arthur Seldon, now advisory director of publications at the Institute of Economic Affairs, for finding the notion that the social services are here to stay as degrading, not ennobling, and Lord Hailsham for having asked some of the right questions, such as the extent to which old age should be self-financed.

'Conservatives surely must strive for a large reduction, in the long run, of the public social services,' Howe continues. 'The State must, of course, accept the permanent responsibility of caring for those who cannot provide for themselves. Plainly, too, it will have to play a leading part in the improvement of our environment ... And the State must not be reluctant to take on other pioneering tasks. Even in a prosperous society necessary claims on public expenditure can only be met if the social services, as we have come to know them, are drastically refashioned, so that their claims are diminished. Over the whole field of social policy our firm aim should therefore be a reduction in the role of the State ... We must ensure that the existing services have built into them the mechanism that is necessary to enable them to contract. People who are able and willing to provide for the health and education of their families should be in every way encouraged to do so.'

Social benefits such as family allowances and pensions should go only to those whose need could not be questioned, he added. There should be compulsory but not necessarily State insurance schemes for all who could afford to pay their way. Private insurance should be actively encouraged possibly by tax concessions, because these would allow people to use part of their earnings to provide for a need which the general taxpayer would otherwise have to meet. But the State might need to devise an insurance scheme for the uninsurable.

Casting an eye over a wider field, Howe went on to discuss education vouchers and even suggested that parents with incomes above a certain level might contribute, say, £5 or £10 per annum to their children's State school. School meals and milk also received his attention. 'There can be no good reason for not charging parents with the full economic cost of this service, accompanied by an extension of the present system of free or subsidized meals for children whose parents cannot afford the full price,' he wrote. 'This surely would be a legitimate burden to place upon increasingly prosperous citizens. If half the £60 million spent each year on this service could be saved, we could afford to double the scale of the hospital building programme. (This was published in 1961, well before the days of great inflation.) Most parents can afford to feed their children. The State alone can build new hospitals.' Another minefield he tackled briefly was the health service and suggested that people should be able to contract out and qualify for a reduction in their income tax equivalent to the average cost per head of the service, provided they proved they were insured adequately elsewhere.

The words and ideas were spinning forth from his pen, mainly in the early hours of the morning, sometimes with members of the particular research group present. 'Shall we do another chapter?' he would say at two or three in the morning and the ordinary mortals, who were and still are his friends, would wonder how they could conceivably survive their normal working day. Howe of course also had his family and career as a barrister. But, if necessary, he could always absorb and retain the essence of his briefs when he got up and made a cup of coffee at six.

6

Ideological Warfare

In the meantime the Bow Group was flexing its political muscles for new ventures and in October 1957 invited the Prime Minister, the Rt Hon Harold Macmillan to launch the new quarterly *Crossbow*, which shot the idea of a world refugee year into the area of political debate and almost immediate acceptance. The publication also had tremendous impact on the group itself. More than 10,000 copies of the first issue were printed, £2,000 from Sir Edward Hulton and the efforts of Peter Cooper, a Howe friend from Cambridge then working for Hulton Press, led to huge publicity and new members surged forward. The small research organization was transformed into a major influence in politics, particularly the politics of the right.

Geoffrey Howe was one of two joint managing directors of the new Bow Publications and, in the unavoidable absence of James Lemkin, the chairman and his co-managing director, performed the welcoming ceremony for the Prime Minister at the Constitutional Club. It was quite a simple speech. 'The Bow Group, we hope, is an intellectual home for young people who care enough about politics to think,' Howe said. 'The second feature of the group is that we are, by our nature, a contemporary organization of contemporary Conservatives. We are not old enough to look back nostalgically to things in earlier years, and regret what was or what might have been. We are not old enough to stand in the contemporary world and regret the problems which face us. Sometimes they may be baffling but I think I can say quite honestly that we are excited by them: hopeful and anxious and happy to try and tackle those problems – rather than spending our life moaning and looking backwards over our shoulders.

'The third thing is this: and this is perhaps what we try to be, rather than what we are. We try, in our pamphlets and in our work, to be radical and honest; to go back humbly enough to scratch when we consider particular problems and to think out the solutions for ourselves. And in our short history we have produced what some people regard as radical pamphlets on a number of problems. The pamphlet which we produced on the reform of rent control foreshadowed the Government's own Act and we are brash enough – and foolish enough – to think that where the Government departed from our own proposals they were misguided.' (That pamphlet was, of course, written by Howe and Colin Jones, the first editor of *Crossbow*.)

After mentioning another pamphlet which had also proved more radical than subsequent government action, he added: 'We are young enough and misguided enough to wish that our elders in politics had the courage of our convictions.'

Mr Macmillan said that he had never been able to persuade any prime minister to participate in the launching ceremony of one of his projects. Of *Crossbow* he added: 'You do not say in which general direction this formidable weapon, the medieval equivalent of a ballistic missile, is to be fired. I am not simple enough to expect that I shall not be – from time to time – one of its principal targets. What gives me fortitude in contemplating this prospect is the thought that the firing will be done by young men who, though they may occasionally and perhaps properly be angry, are facing the problem of the post-war world with a progressive Conservative faith. I do not suppose that the Bow Group will suffer from an excess of orthodoxy. But who am I to complain if, with an average age of twenty-seven (even Geoffrey Howe was only thirty), the Bow Group should from time to time reveal a rebellious air – even a lack of proper respect for your elders? You would probably retort by reference to my own heretical past. Anyway wild oats, political and otherwise, are best sown in youth. They may be painful, even dangerous, in middle age.'

It was time for celebration. The new quarterly meant that the group had a continuous outlet for ideas which would hopefully attract the attention of the national press more consistently than occasional pamphlets, no matter how thoroughly researched or competent. Tim Raison took over from Colin Jones and in 1960 Geoffrey Howe, the first non-journalist editor, from him. The original intention had been to find another journalist for this exacting, potentially influential, but voluntary role. However Howe wanted the job and, backed by Tom Hooson and Russell Lewis, took it on. Since his tenure, Bow Group chairmen have quite frequently become editors of *Crossbow*, including David Howell, Leon Brittan, Patricia Hodgson, now head of the BBC's policy and planning unit, and Peter Lloyd, Tory MP for Fareham.

When Geoffrey Howe took over, he immediately launched new features and set in hand a re-design. He also appointed an editorial board including a number of journalists: Len Beaton, Richard Bing, Adam Fergusson, Judy Hillman, Godfrey Hodgson, David Howell and former *Crossbow* editor, Colin Jones. Adam Fergusson, then with *The Times*, an MEP for West Strathclyde between 1979 and 1984, has recently been working for Sir Geoffrey in the Foreign Office as special adviser on European affairs. The literary editors were Anne Johnson and Susan Le Roux. The editorial board would meet every three months on a Sunday evening in the Chinese Lotus House in the Edgware Road. Howe would arrive with an outline plan for the next issue and members of the articulate team would pitch in with comments and ideas, the chemistry of personality and brainstorm developing and creating a new head of steam for themes and issues – and regular press comment.

Many articles read as well today as they did then, although the nature of the argument is by now much better understood. Take the first issue for example. In an editorial on dynamic conservatism, *Crossbow* called for a clear statement and ceaseless reiteration of the duties and objectives of the western alliance. The peoples of the West needed to be persuaded that, if they were to avoid the harsh reality of nuclear war, the merits of their way of life must be explained and extended. A multi-racial, multi-lingual, multi-credal society devoted to liberty under the law must be built with closer and more sophisticated political consultation. A British Tory government must strive for real and effective integration with Europe; adopt a generous aid programme; and press for the creation of a world security force. 'We should be alert for any opportunity to achieve the controlled reduction of armaments on both sides of the Iron Curtain,' the section on foreign affairs concluded.

Domestically 'the Tory Government should decisively reduce the role of the state in social policy,' it contained. 'More and more people are able (and should be obliged) to pay for personal and family services, so that public funds can be released for true public needs. Any future increase in state pensions should be confined to those that are paid for by contributions. Supplements at the expense of the taxpayer should be given to those who privately insure against accident, sickness or retirement. A percentage of the cost of state education should be recouped in contributions from those who are able to afford it. At least half of the £60 million spent currently on school meals and milk could be recovered in the same way. New legislation should ensure that housing subsidies go only to those who cannot pay an economic rent.' Such savings had a purpose. They would create elbow room for two vital changes: sharp reductions in direct taxation and selective expansion of public investment. 'It will be economically disastrous if the most talented and enterprising Britons continue to be taxed so much more harshly than their Russian and American counterparts. New sources of indirect taxation could on the other hand be tapped – soft drinks, confectionery or meals eaten out for example. Our tax structure is in many ways the result of historical accident. Simplification and rationalization is long overdue. Public expenditure needs to be dramatically expanded in those sectors where the individual is necessarily unable to provide for himself.'

According to *Crossbow*, the target of fifty-five miles of motorway a year was a bare minimum and the British motorist as willing as Americans to pay tolls for a modern highway system. Modern hospitals, particularly for mental health, were another outstanding need and large-scale urban renewal should be the final Tory objective. 'The major successes in post-war Britain – Lansbury, Coventry and the new towns

49

– have all been won by public enterprise. By contrast, large tracts of urban America are being renewed by a combination of public and private endeavour. Bold public plans should be prepared for the renewal, by guided private enterprise, of several large areas of urban blight.' This issue of *Crossbow* appeared in the autumn of 1960. It also included a housing survey on car, telephone and television ownership in two streets of council housing in Coventry; the need for attracting private enterprise into the business of building homes to let; election expenses; a radical rethink of the health service; the influence of the mass media and a square deal for Tory Party agents.

By January 1961, *Crossbow* was calling for a free world economy and the possibility of transforming the International Monetary Fund into a central bank of central banks. ('The United States has so far avoided any really drastic measures to meet its persistent foreign exchange deficit. How long can this go on?'). It continued: 'The peoples of the West need to be told again and again that they have got peace of a kind and that even the preservation of this will demand continued patience and sacrifice ... Disarmament agreements can be negotiated, particularly if an intelligent public opinion can be created and maintained. Close relations between heads of states are an essential insurance against accident. The dangers of a widening gap between East and West are far more serious than the risks of arms control. Britain must take the lead in integrating the alliance; and she must continue to insist on the need to strive for settlements with the Communist world.' There spoke the future Foreign Secretary.

In the autumn of 1961, *Crossbow* was calling for the best brains in the country to concentrate on the single task of streamlining the economic machine so as to make capitalism work better than the collectivist system of the East. Industry must be allowed and obliged to run itself and individuals encouraged to provide for their own welfare. It was the proper role for politicians to plan the strategy for the kind of society and then let the economic experts chart the course. Other ideas in this issue included the need for ministerial sabbatical fortnights to give them time to think even when in office and, as part of a major theme on old age, a call for an old people's Christmas. Loneliness could be solved by society, *Crossbow* claimed, if only one in every five persons were to adopt just one old person, at least for the festive season.

In the spring, Howe, under his own name rather than the semi-anonymity of the editorial column, pressed for freedom for shopkeepers to be allowed to fix their own opening times with unions left to negotiate actual working hours. The following summer *Crossbow* tackled the subject of the environment including the need for decent cities and the preservation of open countryside. At a time when new towns were primarily public initiatives, *Crossbow* suggested the possibility of private development corporations, a scheme for the compulsory pooling of private freeholds and the appointment of a committee to consider a tax on undeveloped site values. In the spring of 1962, Howe handed *Crossbow* on to his successor, David Howell.

At that time in the Bow Group no member had passed the portal into the much coveted House of Commons and no one knew who was going to succeed in political terms. Indeed, only a very few had reached even half their allotted three score years and ten and the official age barrier for Bow Group membership. However it was quite clear to Ron Needs, who had known Geoffrey Howe in the army and who became the group's honorary secretary for a number of years and later ran the business side of *Crossbow*, that there were two types of members – people like Geoffrey Howe, Tom Hooson and Michael Heseltine, who were going to make a political career, and those who simply enjoyed the intellectual challenge of political research and debate and the chance to make friends.

'Geoffrey was quite clear in his mind, I am sure, at that stage that that was what he was going to do and the whole of what he was doing was geared to making an impact in political circles, even though he was at the same time aiming to develop his career in the law,' he says. 'That was why, even though he was not yet in Parliament, one could speculate that he could be prime minister. I think he had and has an extraordinary brain.' Such speculation about the potential political success of Bow Group officers was always a lively topic for after-dinner discussion and it was common ground that Geoffrey Howe would reach high office. However, there were other candidates as well. Ron Needs still has a scrap of paper from the late 1950s stating that Fred Tuckman, now MEP for Leicester, backs David Hennessy (Lord Windlesham) to be a cabinet minister in twenty years (he was leader of the House of Lords from 1973 to 1974). There was £1 on that bet, while Needs had 5s on James Lemkin becoming a junior cabinet minister. James Lemkin did fight the two seats of Chesterfield and Cheltenham – but unsuccessfully – and eventually devoted his political energies for thirteen years to the Greater London Council where he became Opposition chief whip at the end of the Livingstone era. Needs and Fred Tuckman saw Russell Lewis as a future under-secretary, while Heseltine did not feature in their political crystal ball at all.

The Bow Group, then housed in cramped quarters on the site of the future Centre Point, was run for a good deal of this time by Jenny Raven. She was to marry John Wakelin, a Bow Group member who later became headmaster of Hinchingbrooke School, Huntingdon. 'Everybody was always talking about him,' she says of Howe. 'The first evening I met him was at the Constitutional Club and I realized then that what everybody said was true. Geoffrey Howe was an outstanding person.' She was involved in a similar exercise in political futures forecasting on a country weekend at Church Stretton which placed Howe firmly in the role of Home Secretary.

And in an article in *Mayfair* magazine written in 1969 about a future leadership contest in 1984, Reginald Watts, also a former Bow Group chairman, said that Howe, whom he described as 'one of the party's great intellectual forces', had started out as favourite but lost to Nicholas Scott (in 1988 Minister of Social Security, following a long period in Northern Ireland). According to Watts, Howe had by then been successively Minister of Land Use, Education and Social Services and finally Home Secretary. As is normally the way, in the real world he has held four very different appointments – Solicitor-General, Minister for Trade and Consumer Affairs, Chancellor of the Exchequer and Foreign Secretary.

No one at that stage seemed to think in terms of either Chancellor of the Exchequer or Foreign Secretary. 'My main recollection was his fantastic memory for the smallest detail and an absolute phenomenal capacity for work,' says Mrs Wakelin. 'I think he had a natural thirst for work and accomplishment and was always looking for the next challenge along the line. I don't remember him as an idealist particularly; perhaps a natural reformer. A trained mind for mastering a brief quickly and enormous energy and stamina. He was known for being able to function on three to four hours' sleep. He didn't lose his temper or get overheated but kept a sense of proportion and had a ready sense of humour. He wouldn't make enemies because he didn't put people down but skilfully and in a low key would argue the opposite case.'

During this period, friendships were cemented into the fabric of many members' lives. Leon Brittan first made his mark in London politics at the Bow Group, travelling as a student from Cambridge to meetings at the Constitutional Club and amazing graduate members with his self-confidence from the floor as he held forth, thumbs tucked under his jacket lapels. He is a very close friend of the Howes to this day.

Rosemary Wolff is another. When her husband, Michael, died suddenly while cycling on holiday at a health farm in 1975, Geoffrey Howe, together with a group of friends, including Lord Carrington and Sir William Rees-Mogg, then editor of *The Times* and subsequently chairman of the Arts Council of Great Britain, set up a trust fund to ensure his family could complete, as planned, the purchase of their home. Michael Wolff, a former journalist, had recently lost his job as Director General of Central Office in the aftermath of Margaret Thatcher's election as leader of the Tory Party. That was a contest in which Howe, knighted in 1970 and cabinet member of the Heath administration, had taken part and first staked his claim for the highest office in the land. Sir Geoffrey became guardian of the two Wolff children, Lucy and Claudia, who, with their mother, almost became part of the Howe family at Fentiman Road, Lambeth and later in the official Whitehall residences. Elspeth Howe was to become known as Other Mother and Geoffrey as Further Father.

Ten years later, another great Bow Group friend Tom Hooson was to die of cancer. The first Conservative MP for Brecon and Radnor, a man with a lovely sense of humour as well as a good deal of melancholy, he had mainly worked in advertising in London, New York and Paris and finally settled back in London as Director General of the Periodical Publishers

Association. Geoffrey gave a generous and moving memorial address at St Margaret's, Westminster, remembering in particular their joint Bow Group pamphlet on Wales. Foreign Office associates say he is particularly good on such, mainly unrecorded, occasions when he sheds the dry substance of political policy debate for personal expression and feeling.

'I shall never forget the enthusiasm that he brought to that task,' he said of Hooson. 'And the eye for detail, often transmitted to me on scruffy, energetic scraps of paper. Of the 199 footnotes in that pamphlet Tom contributed almost all of them. And all the Welsh quotations. I remember how he was determined that we should finish the pamphlet by the end of a bank holiday weekend in 1959. And how he kept us working through the Monday night, so that when Elspeth emerged at 6 am in the morning to begin heating the milk for our two-month-old twins she was astonished – although not really surprised – to find Tom still on the premises, as fresh and energetic as ever.

'He proved to be a perfect constituency MP, perhaps a little to the surprise of his friends. For in his early days, Tom sometimes seemed to allow little for human imperfection, for the grit of obstinacy, ignorance or sentiment that men and women drop even into the best calibrated machines. He liked, and was liked by, people individually, but sometimes seemed not to understand them collectively. It is one of the great sadnesses of Tom's early death that this is exactly what his constituency life had revealed to him in his later years. All the testimony to his care and consideration, extending to the last weeks and days of his life, shows how his organizing genius had also been flooded with humanity.

'He seemed to know most of his constituents by name, from the post mistress to the milkman in literally hundreds of villages. Soon after his first election he stepped from his Land Rover into the heart of a small village and began announcing over his loudhailer: "This is Tom Hooson, your local Member of Parliament". When one villager asked with surprise: "Is there an election on then?", he was quickly made to realize that the people of Brecon and Radnor would see Tom Hooson between as well as during elections. He was as much at home, and as well-liked, in the Labour parts of his constituency as in the country districts. Perhaps this is because there was, as one of his supporters has told me, "always a bit of a Liberal in him". I suspect Tom would have relished that tribute. A Conservative certainly. But a bit of a Liberal too. Liberal certainly in his friendship, in his enthusiasms, in his hospitality, in his sense of humour – even in his shyness. And liberal too in his courage. All those who saw him in his last tragic days were deeply impressed by that. "You realize, Geoffrey" he told me on the day of our last meeting "that I am in a doom-laden situation". And so, alas it was.'

Tom Hooson, Sir Geoffrey also said, had been determined that the Bow Group was more than a one generation phenomenon and his success could be judged by the fact that he lived to be one of ninety-six Bow Group Members of Parliament. In fact in 1981 Sir Geoffrey, as Chancellor of the Exchequer, was able himself to tell the group's thirtieth anniversary dinner that it had succeeded in capturing the intellectual commanding heights. 'I am convinced,' he said, 'that the cumulative effect of Bow Group speeches and publications has succeeded, as the group's founders hoped it would, in changing the whole climate of opinion. When the group was founded it was, in the words of one of the founders, "not respectable to be Conservative". We would be in danger of tempting fate if we were to claim that it is now "not respectable not to be Conservative". But it is certainly true that in the academic world, in journalism, in intellectual circles generally, the ideas of the free market, individual liberty and the rule of law – all of which then seemed passé – are now back at the centre of the stage. The central themes of political discussion are no longer the Socialist concepts of equality and state planning.' A great deal of this change has stemmed from Howe's own thinking, writing – and doing.

But if some Bow Group friendships are now only remembered with sadness, others continue to evolve. Sir Geoffrey is, for example, godfather to sons of both Judge Bruce Griffiths and William Banks, a solicitor and partner in the same firm as James Lemkin. And the Bow Group did of course set the courtship scene for his own marriage at the age of twenty-six, which was earlier than most of his contemporaries, to Elspeth Rosamund Morton Shand, known as Elspeth to most people, Heppy to her oldest friends, and a political wife extraordinary on the British contemporary scene.

7

On the Home Front

> Poor Sir Geoffrey down at Chevening
> See him on a Friday evening
> Boxes ruddy, in his study
> Maggie's light his guide.
> Now he's flying off to sign a
> Pact with Heppy, his old china
> Was there ever consort finer
> Or a finer bride?

This was the first verse of a song written by a friend from Cambridge days, Alistair Sampson, now an antique dealer and *Punch* columnist, for the Foreign Secretary's sixtieth birthday party held at Chevening in December 1986. It was very much an occasion for family and old friends to eat, drink, make merry and sing. Christopher Cooper, with his group The Loose Chords, sang a special birthday calypso. Solos came from daughter Carrie, Sir Geraint Evans, officially in retirement, Donald Sinden as Good King Wenceslas, the Speaker, the Home Secretary and the Clerk of the House of Commons as the Three Kings plus boisterous choral and carol effects from all under the baton of Peter Cooper. Heppy, the consort finer and a skilful hostess, had set the scene for a memorable and happy celebration.

Geoffrey Howe met Elspeth Shand in 1951 at a London party given by Mary Brock, daughter of Lord Brock and a former schoolfriend from Wycome Abbey. In fact, the Brocks were to become even closer with the family at a later stage when Geoffrey's brother, Colin, married Mary's sister, Angela. Elspeth was working for *Country Fair* magazine, having gone straight from school into secretarial work, as was the norm for young, upper middle-class girls of the day. She later went on to work at the Architectural Association.

On the evening in question Geoffrey Howe was to arrive late from a Bow Group committee meeting and Elspeth Shand was detailed to take him into the kitchen for food and generally to make him feel welcome. She was actually at the party with somebody else. Although Geoffrey was still at Cambridge and had other girlfriends, his first impression was sufficiently important for him to get hold of Elspeth's telephone number the next day and arrange to meet again. Friendship blossomed into engagement later that year.

In retrospect their immediate mutual interest is scarcely surprising since twenty-year-old Elspeth was not just an attractive blonde but intelligent and full of vitality. Geoffrey showed every sign of becoming a successful lawyer and politician, and was fun, witty and kind; aspects of his character which the public rarely see but which friends and associates know well. In any event, two people who were going to make their mark had met and found they had much in common.

Born in 1932, Elspeth was the daughter of Philip Morton Shand, writer of books on food, wine and architecture, a contributor to *The Architectural Review* and founder of the Mars Group on modern architecture. He also helped architect Walter Gropius to escape from Germany. With such a fascinating but bohemian man, life was entertaining but neither conventional nor secure. Elspeth's mother, Sybil, was his fourth wife and it was many years before she met her half-brother Bruce Shand, now Vice Lord Lieutenant of East Sussex and former chairman of a firm of London and Lewes wine merchants. He is the son of Philip Shand's first wife and is fifteen years older than Elspeth. She also has a half-sister, Rosemary (from the second marriage) but, so far as immediate family was concerned, grew up with her elder sister Mary, an interior designer who later married James Stirling. Often known as Big Jim, he has carved out an international reputation as an architect for schemes such as the Stuttgart museum, which in 1986 featured in the Royal Academy's exhibition of work by three of Britain's premier architects – James Stirling, Norman Foster and Richard Rogers. James Stirling was also responsible for the Clore extension to house the Tate Gallery's Turner collection in London and for Liverpool's new Tate Gallery in the North.

Although Elspeth went to Wycombe Abbey, one of the country's best-known girls boarding schools, the family had little ready money, her father having been virtually disowned by his very Victorian parents when he married for the second time. However, a family trust paid for the girls' education. Following evacuation to Oxford during the Second World War, the Shands settled in Bath and her mother took a job in the Admiralty to boost her father's more irregular earnings as a writer. At Wycombe Abbey, Elspeth was a typical schoolgirl of the day with a healthy aptitude and appetite for games, especially lacrosse and cricket, and only really began to take any real interest in academic work in the sixth form. There was no thought of university. That was to come many years after, when her three children had grown up, Geoffrey was Chancellor of the Exchequer and they were living at No 11 Downing Street. Ever in need of a challenge and without the independent career which by then she had grown to love as deputy chairman of the Equal Opportunities Commission, she went to the London School of Economics. Geoffrey used to joke with friends that he must be the only one who would be spending the night with an LSE student and in 1985 Elspeth added an honours degree in social science and administration to her fairly formidable curriculum vitae.

When the two first met, the future Lady Howe was very much attracted to the arts and the theatre, which had formed a key ingredient to Geoffrey's enjoyment of Cambridge. However Elspeth quickly realized the underlying importance of politics in Geoffrey's life-plan and therefore their friendship. She became equally passionately involved, and an active member of the Bow Group.

Geoffrey was called to the Bar in 1952 and the following year on August 29, during the legal vacation, they were married at St Peter's, Vere Street. They had a reception at the Wimpole

Street home of John and Peggy Seymour, whose daughter Kay was one of Elspeth's closest friends at school, and a honeymoon in Ibiza.

Their first home was a basement flat in 39 Wimpole Street, with two rooms, kitchen and bathroom and a small patio. Their first child, Caroline, was born in 1955. Geoffrey's mother had been a twin and their twins, Amanda and Alec, arrived in 1959. Caroline was to become a singer, Amanda a lawyer and Alec press officer to the Campaign for Nuclear Disarmament. It was a role which could easily have proved embarrassing for his father as Foreign Secretary and did cause tension within the family – but tolerance and a belief in the rights of individuals to different views avoided a major clash. As the family grew, the Howes moved into a larger flat at 20 Upper Wimpole Street, buying the whole house with a mortgage from the family, living in the bottom half and renting out the top. From there they went to Fentiman Road in Lambeth in the vanguard of political and more general gentrification of the back streets of Vauxhall.

For about ten years the family took the children and the two grandmothers on holiday to a farm at Boisroger, near Coutances, Normandy, often joining up with Michael and Rosemary Wolff and their two children. Leon Brittan, then unmarried, was another friend who fitted happily into this scene. Geoffrey would talk in French to Monsieur Michel, the farmer, about the practical effects of the Common Market; the English children learnt to milk cows by hand and the Howes taught the farm children to swim. Geoffrey filmed family adventures, later editing the material into shape and providing a sound track commentary and musical background as he had done in his Winchester school days. For a family whose father was preoccupied with work and politics, this annual retreat was enormously important as a period of recreation as well as recreation and there was tremendous distress when the farmer and his wife were tragically drowned in 1973. An era had ended and nowadays, with security and privacy more of a problem, Sir Geoffrey and Lady Howe tend to borrow a house in the south of France. For all his long hours and addiction to work, he loves holidays, time off and the chance to relax.

At home, music is a staple diet to aid the concentration. Geoffrey told Michael Parkinson in 1986 on the BBC radio programme *Desert Island Discs* that the sound of music was 'an inescapable part of the background of a Welshman'. Certainly it has been an inescapable part of Geoffrey's working background from Cambridge days, when he fantasized with Richard Stone about the possibility of pirate radio well before Radio Caroline invaded the country's protected air waves.

Geoffrey Howe's taste was, and is, catholic. As a potential castaway for the by now well-populated mythical desert island, his choice of records included a Welsh male-voice choir recording, Noel Coward's *Mad Dogs and Englishmen*, parts of Mozart's *Magic Flute* and Rachmaninov's *Second Piano Concerto*, the Beatles' *Eleanor Rigby*, the Glenn Miller Orchestra playing *Tuxedo Junction* and Cliff Richard's *Summer Holiday*. He also chose an entertaining and strangely moving oddity – Miss Beatrice Harrison on the cello playing Dvořák to accompany a nightingale, which was recorded before the Second World War in woodlands in his constituency. Sir Geoffrey's personal luxury was a computer bridge game with solar batteries with *The Good Food Guide* to complement Shakespeare and the Bible. It was his second opportunity to present a personal choice of records. In 1977, when he was shadow Chancellor, he appeared on Radio Three's *Man of Action*, a programme which did away with the interview and left the man in the spotlight to knit his life together with music. Again there was the obeisance to Wales with the hymn *Aberystwyth*, sung at the funerals of his grandfather and his parents; *Finlandia* by Sibelius, which he first heard as a boy in Ostend with Aunti Lil; the *Pilgrim's March* from Mendelssohn's *(Italian) Fourth Symphony*, which he played on the piano with his school house orchestra; plus Tchaikovsky, Mozart, Ravel, Verdi, Rossini, Donizetti, the Beatles' *Penny Lane*; Julian Slade's *We Said We Wouldn't Look Back* from *Salad Days*, and Beethoven's *Ninth (Choral) Symphony*, which was played at the Fanfare for Europe to celebrate Britain's accession to Europe. 'The bright hopes of those days must seem a little tarnished today, but by no means inevitably,' he concluded. 'The peoples of the continent of which we are a part still have the capacity to display those qualities of energy and civilization which have inspired our contribution to the history of the world.'

With such a demanding life, it is as well that Lady Howe, wife, mother, political helpmate and hostess, retains so many interests and a healthy independence of outlook. However, while friends used teasingly to forecast that she would be elected to the House of Commons before him, she always manages in public to remain just outside the limelight and play the expected supporting role with consummate skill. She listens intently to speeches, the contents of which she knows full well, and laughs, particularly during an election campaign, at jokes which are currently in her husband's repertoire. In 1966 when he was defending (and lost) Bebington, Geoffrey used coyly to react to Labour gibes about thirteen wasted years of Tory rule with a remark to the effect that he had been married for thirteen and: 'They haven't been wasted, have they darling?' Elspeth would look suitably surprised and pleased. She constantly protects his interests, attends his parliamentary questions and major speeches in the House of Commons, quietly sits in on overseas press conferences and watches television performances with a constructively critical eye, telling him where he has come across well and where perhaps he might improve in the future. Although he has recently begun to enunciate more clearly with more colour in his voice, even well-wishing observers may wonder whether her commentary over the years has been too kind or her husband too stubborn to accept a real need for change in the presentation of his ideas, particularly in short interviews on radio or television.

When Geoffrey was selected in televised competition with Christopher Chataway as candidate for the safe Conservative Reigate constituency following the loss of his Cheshire seat, the wives were also invited to make a short contribution. Afterwards, some local association members came away saying that Mrs Howe's carefully non-political speech won him the seat. Indeed some people at first acquaintance think she is the power house driving his ability. But such judgement is superficial and arises from his generally comfortable, genial and non-aggressive demeanour. 'Inside that Winnie-the-Pooh exterior, there's a very stubborn man,' says one friend. According to another: 'Geoffrey's success is because of his own personality.

There is ambition in the man. Ambition is quite a creditable human characteristic and a most constructive thing if properly applied – and I think it is in his case.'

Certainly Elspeth Howe has been extremely careful that her own roles are complementary and, if needs be, she gives way when his needs demand. Her appointment as deputy chairman of the Equal Opportunities Commission by the Labour Government in 1975 well fitted her ability and personal ambition to prove that she was someone who could campaign, manage and organize on her own behalf and in her own right. It was an area on which she, and indeed Sir Geoffrey, had and have very firm views. But in 1979, when his appointment as Chancellor of the Exchequer laid the seeds for direct conflict between the Government and the EOC in the European Court, she decided she must resign. It was a tough decision and one made no easier by the parallel difficulty of taking up otherwise suitable alternative offers. While she waited restlessly in the wings of Downing Street, virtually every suggestion or proposal was found politically unsuitable in view of her husband's key economic role. And potential appointments to the ranks of the great and the good were equally impossible, regardless of her qualifications, because promotion might seem like nepotism. The loss of income, purpose and career were all sore points and eventually Lady Howe signed on instead at the London School of Economics to take a belated degree, nonetheless accompanying Sir Geoffrey, who was by then Foreign Secretary, on numerous foreign trips during her two final years. In 1986 she accepted a new paid role, this time in the private sector as a non-executive director on the Woolworth board.

Always an ardent volunteer, Elspeth Howe has been for many years chairman of an Inner London juvenile court, is president of the Women's Gas Federation, the Federation of Recruitment and Employment Services, and the Peckham Settlement, and a member of the Council of the National Association for the Care and Resettlement of Offenders and the Policy Studies Institute. Like her husband she has served on a variety of committees including the Lord Chancellor's Advisory Committee on the appointment of magistrates for Inner London, another on legal aid and the Briggs Committee on Nursing. A former chairman and governor of several schools in Tower

Hamlets, she was also co-opted as a Conservative for three years to the Inner London Education Authority. And she is a former vice-chairman of the Conservative London Area Women's Advisory Committee and member of the Conservative Women's National Advisory Committee.

Whenever suitable, Elspeth Howe travels with Sir Geoffrey overseas. At international conferences she mixes easily with other wives listening to their points of view and quietly selling Britain. On special visits, she somewhat startled embassy staff in the early days when she suggested her programme should include a visit to the local prison. Obviously this was no conventional Foreign Secretary's spouse, but they were quickly won over by her lively interest and good humour, and nowadays accept such excursions as the norm. She has also taken an active interest in the choice of Foreign Office gifts to visiting dignitaries bringing knowledge and influence to bear in favour of quality British design.

Since 1979 the Howes have lived in London in the political, if grander, equivalent of the tied cottage, leaving Fentiman Road for a maisonette in No 11 or more strictly No 12 Downing Street and then on to the upper floors of the Nash terrace at No 1 Carlton Gardens. Lady Howe has had to learn to stamp her personality on government property mainly through a goodly scattering of pictures and family photographs (including Sir Geoffrey following Prince Philip through the massed ranks of terracotta soldiers in China, and with Margaret Thatcher on the Tory Party conference platform with the Prime Minister's signed congratulations at the bottom). In addition there are cartoons, *Spitting Image* reproductions and a mass of mementoes and curios presented on the diplomatic round.

The Howes have always enjoyed entertaining friends on Sunday evenings, which is the one night of the week which fitted in with the demands of the Commons, the constituency and, while he was a barrister and QC, cases spent largely out of town on the South Wales circuit. In the early days of her marriage, Elspeth astounded friends with her general competence by poaching a sizeable salmon, for lack of a proper fish kettle, in a washing machine. She simply heated the water up and then turned it off to allow the fish, wrapped in foil, to cook in its own steam. If the story comes up these days,

Geoffrey is quite likely to reminisce about his bachelor days when he shared a flat with Patrick Jenkin and the time the monthly haggis blew from the pressure cooker onto the kitchen ceiling.

The Howes have developed a happy tradition of mixing friends and contacts from a wide range of backgrounds. At Fentiman Road there might be ten people, at Downing Street perhaps fourteen, with the men in traditional fashion left briefly with port or brandy before rejoining the women for coffee. Unlike many high-fliers, who have too little time for friends from the past, the Howes retain and seem to need regular contact with their roots. They also make time for other generations, assembling the godchildren, for example, to see Geoffrey rehearse (to much merry comment) his television budget speech from a room in Downing Street. One godchild was apparently very put out when his godfather avoided the subsequent washing-up because the woman from next door at No 10 popped in and asked if he would just come over and have a word – and he left immediately.

Pressures on time at the Foreign Office – with major conferences, visits abroad, negotiations and the continual round of ministerial meetings at Brussels, not to mention the regular diplomatic circuit with dinners, luncheons and receptions – are much greater and make such gatherings less frequent. But the Howes have the use of Chevening: a beautiful comfortable country house usually attributed to Inigo Jones in red brick with white trim and pilasters and set in 3,500 acres of parkland in Kent.

In 1967 on the death of the seventh Earl Stanhope, the house became one of the more extraordinary tied properties of the land with a series of possible occupants, set out by law in the 1959 Chevening Estate Act. The Prime Minister has the pleasant task of offering what has currently become a coveted grace and favour residence for cabinet ministers, although Prince Charles was the Royal nominee for six years before he married and bought a country home in Gloucestershire. Since the Prime Minister already has Chequers available as a rolling English countryside retreat within easy range of London, other senior ministers can have the opportunity of enjoying the ambience of an English country house with few of the normal financial worries. The trustees employ a small staff to look after the house and garden and the minister and his family and friends learn to love the Stanhopes. Since 1981 the chosen have all been Foreign Secretaries – Lord Carrington, followed by Francis, now Lord, Pym, and since 1983, Sir Geoffrey. If it ever should happen that no cabinet minister or relevant Royal should want Chevening, the house has first to be offered to the Canadian High Commissioner, then the United States Ambassador and finally, if all were to spurn the chance of such gracious living, it would pass into the hands of the National Trust.

It is obviously a splendid place to hold occasional meetings in a more relaxed atmosphere than can be offered in government buildings in and around Whitehall, and the Chancellor also regularly withdraws for a budget planning weekend with his officials. Here once again the Howes, when their timetable permits, have opened wide the doors to their friends as well as official guests. On a fairly regular basis they invite perhaps eight people for a weekend which starts at 12.30 pm on Saturday and ends soon after lunch on Sunday. They may be fellow Conservative MPs or peers, friends from Cambridge or Bow Group days, the law, or business, the media or the Foreign Office. Upstairs, guests find their rooms complete with Stanhope portraits, views over the lake or the formal maze, and a number of books carefully chosen to tempt their known or supposed interests. Drinks are taken in the drawing room under the world-weary gaze of Lord Chesterfield and lunch in a dining room where yet more Stanhope connections watch from the walls. The fare is simple with Sir Geoffrey, as Foreign Secretary, the first to be served. After lunch, guests are given their marching orders, unless they prefer to accompany the Foreign Secretary when he drives up later after an hour or so at work. The route curves up into a beech wood at the top of the North Downs, and Summit, the successor Jack Russell to Budget and Quintin Dog, scampers after real and imaginary rabbits. Sir Geoffrey walks back down with the group to an old-fashioned English tea of scones and cake and leads a tour of the magnificent library with its 19,000 books and the chance to see a hand-written Disraeli bread-and-butter tour-de-verse. Once again the Foreign Secretary retires to work until candlelit dinner followed by bridge or team snooker. The Howes enjoy games and play to win. When the guests go to bed, the host returns to his study yet again.

Sunday breakfast is the best of cooked British with sufficient newspapers for all to choose silence if they so wish. Church is optional, as is a walk round the lake with its resident Canada geese, trumpeter swans and ducks. Lady Howe occasionally fishes there with some success, but tends to throw her catches back. A further ten guests, including one ambassador, arrive for lunch. Such an innovation originally caused quite a stir in the Foreign Office which was concerned that some ambassadors might never find themselves at this informally formal, but friendly, gathering in the country. Eventually commonsense won and over a period of time a number do enjoy the chance of meeting an interesting cross-section of British society. In true British puritan tradition the Howes bear the costs of their personal, as opposed to their public, entertainment. There are few airs and graces in this grace and favour setting, only the constant pressure and obvious presence of security which nowadays surrounds those who achieve the higher rungs of political success.

8

In and Out of the House

To reach the top echelons of government and the problems, pressures and pleasures of power takes time as well as talent. It also takes the ability to withstand popular rejection by constituency parties as a potential candidate and by constituencies as a whole as parliamentary swings unseat the marginal member. Geoffrey Howe was no exception in this morale-toughening process in which, simply for ambition to survive, all failure must be accepted as temporary. If anything he took longer than most to establish himself in a safe seat but, probably as a result of the Bow Group, Conservative Political Centre and other policy publications, moved faster, when he did finally take his place in the House of Commons, from the back to the front bench.

His first exposure as a Tory candidate occurred during Bow Group days in the 1955 General Election. At twenty-eight and recently married, he needed to build up his practice as a barrister and Aberavon, which included his home town, was an ideal seat on which to begin to test his political metal. His wife Elspeth, by then pregnant with the first of their three children, was one of three Howe women who canvassed the streets of Port Talbot; the others being his mother and Auntie Lil. This South Wales steelworks constituency was, of course, solidly Labour, a tradition which even extended to the Conservative working men's club and Howe had to insist on his right to enter. Frequently he was told by people that they wished he was Labour. While Howe admired certain aspects of the Welsh Labour movement – including its local passion for home ownership, quality in education and patriotism – he placed far too much faith in individual freedom and choice ever to have opted for collectivism and centralized state control. In May 1955 the new Conservative candidate, subsequently described as Mr Richard Howe in the election yearbook published by *The Times*, increased his party's share by some 800 votes to 12,706. His successful Labour opponent, W.G.Cove, received 29,003, sixty-nine and a half per cent of the poll.

After a futile attempt in Poplar for the London County Council – Bow Group territory but solid Labour – in October 1959 Geoffrey Howe was once again back on the Aberavon hustings. Again he was defeated, this time by another barrister, John Morris, subsequently Secretary of State for Wales with the last Wilson Cabinet. Howe pushed up his personal total by fifty-six in the face of a third Plaid Cymru candidate who attracted some 3,000 votes. Nationally the Conservatives increased their majority. In a four-page election newspaper, which he wrote and edited, Howe set out his personal credo. There is very little, if anything, he would wish to change. Under the heading 'I'm no yes-man', he stated: 'The most important quality in Britain's next generation of politicians should be honesty – ruthlessly realistic intellectual honesty. Too many politicians have become accustomed to wearing a quite different face in public from that which they wear in private. Too many have adopted an attitude of resigned helplessness in face of a party policy which they dislike. Too many have grown accustomed to the empty shadow-boxing of our present parliamentary procedure – and its growing detachment from the people of the country. Too many have never tried to comprehend the widespread feeling of cynicism and despair at the whole business of party politics. And far too many of the electorate have ceased to hope for any determination, any reality, any integrity of purpose from the politicians.'

Possibly, he added, this was an odd way to begin an election address and he hoped that people would not think him immodest.

Howe continued: 'I am not someone who believes in "My party – right or wrong". The Tory Party has not got a monopoly of truth in politics. No more is it fair to suggest that the Labour Party is barren of good ideas. On the contrary, I believe that the leaders of both parties and most of their supporters are each trying in their own way to do what they think best for the country.

'I am not the kind of person who accepts ready-made answers to political questions. I like to think things out for myself – starting from first principles. It's in that spirit that I've done most of my political work so far: I've written pamphlets on three subjects – local government, housing and the future of Wales. In each of those pamphlets you'll find views that are sometimes out of line with Tory Party policy – though most of them are good Conservatism. Just as I have not been afraid to depart from the party line in print, so I should be willing to do so in Parliament – when the merits of the case require it.

'Why then am I a Conservative? Because in British politics today, although one should be free to decide many questions on their merits, one has also to decide on the general nature of the system of government one prefers. And on that central issue I am in no doubt in preferring the Tory solution. Basically I believe that individual happiness and public well-being are best achieved not by some all-wise central plan but by the multiplication of individual opportunity. A single State-directed plan needs only one mistake to go catastrophically wrong. It can so easily become involved in unjustifiable restriction of private liberty. The Conservative policy of lowering taxes and diffusing wealth serves to multiply individual opportunities for doing good to the community. And the best kind of Conservatism is also alert to take specific measures to remove injustice and alleviate hardship. I am convinced that this practical and considered approach is more likely to reconcile prosperity with social justice than the single creed of Socialists in more and more State-ownership.'

Howe asked them to pick the man and not the ticket, not because he had a great idea of his own ability but because he promised, if elected, 'to work hard in politics, to think things out, to get things done and to say and do what I honestly

70

(*Above*) Lloyd George knew Geoffrey's father . . . and his mother. Seen here in the south of France.

(*Right*) Geoffrey and his younger brother Colin with their mother, Lili Howe (left), and their Auntie Lil.

The Howes on holiday in
Belgium. From left to right:
Geoffrey's father, Geoffrey,
Auntie Lil, his brother Colin
and his mother.

(*Left*) Geoffrey as a young boy.

Geoffrey as a new boy at
Winchester in 1940.

On leaving school in 1945.

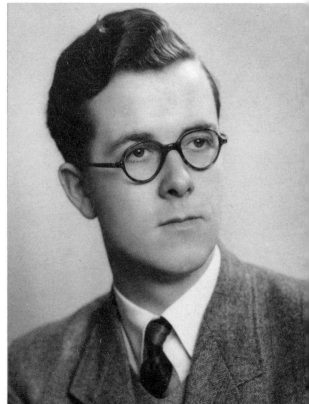

(*Above left*) 2nd Lt. Howe did his national service in the Royal Signals. Seen here on passing out from Catterick (front row, third from right). Ron Needs (front row, second from left) was to meet up with him in the Bow Group.

(*Below left*) A debate in the Cambridge Union with Geoffrey Howe, a committee member, seated on the back bench, second from right.

(*Above*) At a private coal mine in Ebbw Vale on a political speaking tour with fellow Cambridge students including Patrick Jenkin, now a member of the House of Lords (centre back).

A Cambridge University Conservative Association dance with Geoffrey Howe in the centre. Other guests included Norman St John Stevas (fourth from left), now a member of the House of Lords, and Russell Lewis, who like Geoffrey became chairman of the Bow Group, and Richard Stone, now a QC and a Wreck Commissioner (third and fifth from right respectively).

(*Opposite above*) An early Bow Group weekend conference. Geoffrey Howe is sitting in the second row fifth from left. Other faces with a political future or mentioned in the book include: Patrick Jenkin (back row, seventh from left), Norvela Forster, a former MEP (back row, far right), John Biffen (third row, second from left), Beryl Cooper, Richard Stone and Ron Needs (second row, extreme left, fourth and second from right) and Russell Lewis and Fred Tuckman, MEP for Leicester (front row, seventh and eighth from left respectively).

(*Opposite below*) As chairman of the Bow Group, in the group's offices in St Giles-in-the-Field.

His first election campaign with three Howe women boosting his support in Aberavon, a politically hopeless seat for a Tory. From the left, Auntie Lil, his mother and his wife Elspeth, who was expecting their first child.

(*Below*) The Howe family in Dunstable Mews behind their Wimpole Street home . . . with Caroline (left) and twins Amanda and Alec.

believe to be right'. According to his four-point personal plan for the next five years he would: press for the introduction of Queen's scholarships for one-third of all places in public schools; try to simplify the tax system and encourage the spread of savings and home ownership; introduce full industrial injury insurance to entitle everyone to compensation related to pre-accident earnings; and press for the simplification of the law and the removal of out-dated restrictions.

Front page stories highlighted issues of the day – the prospect of steel nationalization, the need for a local by-pass and prices – nylons, blankets and shoes had actually gone down between 1951 and 1959. About twice as many people owned cars and motor cycles and nine million families owned a television and 'despite Socialist opposition – there's a free choice of programmes', he wrote. The country was eating more and better food. In 1951 almost everything had been rationed – one egg, 8d worth of meat and three ounces of butter per week. Average butter consumption per head per week was now six ounces 'just twice as good' (but of course that was before the days when large numbers of people began to wonder just how good butter in fact was for general health). Even the numbers of people taking holidays abroad had doubled to 2,500,000. (In 1985 the figure was 22,000,000 and virtually every household has a television.)

With two election fights under his belt it was time to win selection in at least a winnable, if not a safe, seat. It was no easy task. Geoffrey Howe trailed himself and his achievements before local Conservative committees. His natural low-key, sometimes diffident manner and speeches, packed with well researched but certainly not flamboyant prose, have rarely been designed for speedy emotional appeal. And while local political enthusiasts may like the idea of a Member of Parliament who not only seems to listen but actually absorbs their problems, they may also like to feel there really is fire in the belly and the ability to inspire as well as argue ideas. In addition, the left-wing Bow Group might constantly be breaking new intellectual ground in the making of Tory policy but the party in the country at large, often dominated by self-satisfied local businessmen, county families or women with social pretensions, quite liked the world as it was and were

71

wary of a man with such obvious brains and radical liberal attitudes.

In 1963 Geoffrey was finally adopted by Bebington in Cheshire and the Howes rented a cottage at Malpas to begin to nurse a constituency, which combined Port Sunlight and part of Birkenhead with Liverpool commuter territory and a little of the Cheshire hunting-shooting squirarchy. On 15 October 1964 in a three-cornered fight with the Liberals Geoffrey was elected by a majority of 2,209 to a House of Commons in which Labour had the tiny majority of four and Harold Wilson was prime minister. There was a certain timeless quality about the first Queen's speech Geoffrey was to hear from the backbenches. 'In international affairs it will be the principal purpose of my ministers to seek to reduce East–West tensions ... They will seek to encourage further progress towards disarmament and to contribute to other steps which will permit the East–West conflict to be replaced by international co-operation in promoting peace and security throughout the world.' She went on to reaffirm the Government's support for the defence of the free world, the basic concept of the Atlantic Alliance, the North Atlantic Treaty Organization, the Commonwealth and closer European co-operation. (Britain had yet to join the European Economic Community.) On the domestic front the story now seems more dated, but made much of the strength of sterling and the need to deal with balance of payments difficulties before moving on to more controversial matters such as the public ownership of iron and steel, the hope for co-operation between unions and employers organizations to eliminate restrictive practices, the restoration of rent control and the introduction of the Crown Land Commission.

Geoffrey Howe joined a House of Commons which included as fellow Tory members: Edward Boyle, R. A. Butler, Reginald Maudling, Iain MacLeod, Ernest Marples, Peter Thorneycroft and Christopher Soames who, with the exception of Lord Thorneycroft, are no longer alive. Others included Quintin Hogg (now Lord Hailsham), Margaret Thatcher and a number of Bow Group friends such as John Biffen, who shared the Malpas cottage at weekends, Christopher Chataway, Jock Bruce-Gardyne and Antony Buck. On 11 November 1964, James Callaghan as Chancellor of the Exchequer brought forward a budget designed to tackle balance of payments problems saying he had been shocked to find that the annual deficit was likely to be as high as £800 million. He introduced a fifteen per cent surcharge on most imports, 6d on income tax and a new corporation tax for industry. On 12 November Howe made his maiden speech and dared a small joke at the new Prime Minister's expense by quoting from the Wirral Grammar School magazine. 'A most villainous villain' and 'With more vivacity he should do well', the drama critic had said of a younger Harold Wilson. Geoffrey Howe also paid obeisance to Enoch Powell, whose economic ideas were very influential on his thinking, saying that benefits for all were the enemy of care for the few. Howe pressed for the extension of the means test to school milk, school meals, legal aid and pensions.

In December he was up on his feet again on the subject of protection from eviction. Security of tenure for furnished lettings would, he said, threaten to dry up the supply. In February Howe was pleading for better employment opportunities for the active elderly, more meals on wheels and increased sheltered housing combined with a plea for more diversified housing ownership and management. Even councils, he said, could have different municipal management bodies looking after self-contained estates, begin to develop more flexible rent policies and encourage mobility.

Very soon he was a labour and social services spokesman and pushed out yet another pamphlet: *In Place of Beveridge.* Inflation and rising national prosperity had made formerly adequate pensions seem derisory, he wrote. But increases in the basic pension meant that they no longer related to insurance contributions. 'Do we want, for the foreseeable future and however affluent we may become, to perpetuate a huge machinery whereby the State redistributes such a large proportion of the national income?' Howe asked. 'Do we want, for ever, to fight a series of "pensioneering" elections, with politicians bidding against each other with promises to raise the basic rate? And do we want to sustain for ever the impression that the State is, and should be, willing and able to provide a guaranteed hedge against inflation for all those who have retired – so that inflation itself becomes an inevitable and regularly accepted feature of our way of life? It is this last proposition that most Conservatives are rightly reluctant to accept. What prospect is there of maintaining confidence in any kind of private saving and investment if we live, as we have done since the war, in an economy in which the real value of money is roughly halved in every twenty years. Yet there is good reason to believe that a State-run pension scheme, with its own built-in guarantee to raise pensions in line with any rise in prices, is itself a powerfully inflationary force.' In contrast, Howe boosted the idea of private-sector pensions, transferability and the over-riding need for competition and greatly reduced levels of inflation. 'A society in which more and more people are able to take a larger personal share in deciding the pattern of their standard of living in old age would certainly be more responsible and self-reliant than that in which we live today. A society in which more and more people were able to choose the time at which they could retire and to select the way in which their retirement would be financed would certainly be a freer one than that to which we are accustomed.'

All too soon the Labour Government called an election and in March 1966 Geoffrey Howe was back on the hustings. Capital punishment was one major issue. Always a sensitive subject in Tory circles, Conservative candidates in the Liverpool area decided jointly to avoid confrontation by saying they would all press for a popular referendum and abide by the result. While Howe had supported capital punishment in his Cambridge days, he had not only changed his views but refused to take such a comfortable if slippery path into personal irresponsibility and stood his ground. Questions were planted at every public meeting and each time he stated his belief that Members of Parliament were not delegates and that he was against capital punishment and would not vote for it. One meeting stands out in the memory of friends. A couple of men were creating a rumpus near the front with a noose and placard relating to trade union demands. The crowd was getting out of hand and someone even thought of telephoning the police. When Howe arrived, the normally reasonable lawyer unveiled hidden Welsh depths, spoke sharply, then made everyone laugh and order and good humour returned. A potentially ugly scene was deftly handled. In that election he also constantly compared the low level of health service charges with the much greater amount the British were prepared to spend on pet foods.

His 1966 constituency message kicked off with a list of action areas: lower taxes; the establishment of growth zones; legally enforceable agreements between unions and employers; the introduction of a new industrial court; and entry into Europe at the first favourable opportunity. Little could he have known that he would in due course have the chance himself to steer legislation through the House of Commons on all these fronts, particularly as the country swung firmly to Labour including Bebington. Edwin Brooks, a university geography lecturer, whose majority was 2,337 expressed his delight at winning but also unusually said that it was sad that Geoffrey Howe would not be in the Commons as well, and he hoped he would be back as soon as possible, although of course not in his seat.

To lose is always traumatic and Geoffrey Howe was very disappointed. He had inherited a healthy majority of nearly 10,000 in 1963 and seen it disintegrate as the character of the area began to change. But he had heard early results and knew the swing was too great for there to be any hope of his immediate political survival. He drove back to the cottage to meet up with John Biffen, whose seat was not to be declared until the following day. When those votes were counted, Biffen was still in Parliament. Howe who, as a barrister had become a Queen's Counsel the previous year at the early age of thirty-eight, simply sent his clerk in chambers a telegram: 'Brother, can you spare a dime.'

The dime was multiplied many times over during the next four years. But Howe did not go near the House of Commons. Instead he directed his energies into his work at the Bar where his reputation grew with a series of important briefs. In the political world he became one of the most popular Tory speakers outside the Cabinet and was prepared to journey far and wide, as he also had to in the quest for a new, safer seat. Bebington had become too marginal for a man intent on ministerial achievement.

It was again a long depressing trail of rejection in which he lost out to people like Patrick McNair-Wilson in the New Forest, Dudley Smith at Warwick and Leamington, Sir Brandon Rhys Williams in Kensington and Sir George Sinclair in Dorking where Howe was considered far too left-wing. In the autumn of 1967 however another safe Surrey seat came on the political market with the decision by Sir John Vaughan Morgan (Eton, Oxford and the Guards) to retire as long-standing MP for Reigate. A great deal of attention focused on the choice of candidate since the local Conservative Party organization in this comfortable slice of semi-suburban green belt decided to widen the selection of the new man to 500 paid-up party members instead of the more usual small inner cabal or clique.

The process was perforce drawn out, if not tedious, as the original 263 applicants were heavily pruned, first to a short-list and finally to just two names for the mini election the following June. It has long been normal practice for aspiring politicians to have to show off wives – even husbands – as constituencies try to assess character and suitability behind the skilful personality sales pitch of the eager and ambitious. In the Market Hall at Reigate however the spouses – both wives – were to break platform silence and in so doing possibly break or make their husband's immediate career. The drama of the occasion was heightened by the very different qualities of the two contenders, both deliberately of ministerial potential since the constituency had also decided to back a man who seemed well set for the top echelons of government. On the one side stood Christopher Chataway, thirty-seven, literally a runaway success, an Olympics athelete who briefly held the world 5,000 metres record in 1954, television broadcaster, former MP for Lewisham North for seven years and already boasting junior ministerial experience in education and science. Against him was ranged Geoffrey Howe QC, now forty-one, a political intellectual, former Opposition frontbench spokesman on labour and social services. Both had Bow Group connections with Chataway a party to the *Crossbow* proposal for a world refugee year and Howe a former managing director and editor of the same magazine.

As has happened frequently in Howe's career, some commentators made the mistake of underestimating his skill, strength and ambition because of his mild, seemingly diffident and eminently reasonable, manner. Chataway was the more obvious star and favourite in the press. With the Thames television programme *This Week* recording the choice, Howe spoke of the need for leadership, a healthy economy, entry into Europe and national faith. Chataway concentrated on the quality of life and, of perennial interest just outside London, the need to contain the spread of development within the south-east. Both acquitted themselves well and there was a real sense in which their respective wives could win or lose the battle. They too had to calculate the likely mood, interest and preference of the audience but, above all, remember that each was the potential candidate's wife, not a candidate.

Elspeth Howe, politically knowledgeable and very much involved with young children and voluntary work, spoke very simply. 'For me,' she said, 'I think the most important thing about being an MP's wife is to believe and to realize that what you really are is just an ordinary wife. At home I think that this means trying to keep a calm and stable background for Geoffrey and our three children because politicians do lead a fairly hectic and demanding sort of life and I suspect that they need slightly more love and attention than most other breeds of husband.' There was not a word about her ability and interests. Like her husband, Anna Chataway, was the more obviously glamorous. She spoke of her role as president of the North Lewisham Women's Advisory Committee, made a joke about canvassing and praised her husband and his ideals.

That evening Geoffrey Howe won the constituency delegates' support, some said because of his sincerity, some because he was less slick, some because of his wife's able but clearly supportive role. One local member remembers her father coming back from the meeting and saying they had selected a very nice man called Geoffrey Howe and Mrs Howe, who was called Elspeth, and she was very good. 'My father felt he had come across as a worthwhile person who would take great interest in the constituency and would be more suitable than a glamorous athlete and broadcaster. And his wife was going to be a great asset,' she now says. However when she learnt he was a barrister, she remembered having seen him in a television debate unfashionably defending a woman who sent her children to a private school and thought there might be more to this future MP than met the eye.

The constituency magazine that summer said: 'Those who know Mr Howe well, tell us of his keenness, his inexhaustible energy, his great ability and they prophesy that before very long he will be in the Cabinet and ultimately be the responsible head of one of the most important ministries.' In the same issue, Geoffrey said he could not pretend the process of selection was not alarming and described the final confrontation as gruelling for all the principal performers. 'But then that's as it should be,' he wrote before delivering his first thoughts, which touched on industrial relations but, even twenty years ago, concentrated on a reduced role for the welfare state.

'At the present time it looks like being impossible to keep the growth of welfare spending as a whole down to less than six per cent a year,' Howe wrote. 'Educational spending, in particular, seems bound to increase at something nearer eight per cent a year. Now if we set these figures alongside even the most optimistic forecasts of growth in the economy – say three or even four per cent a year – it is plain that taxes will have to go up in order to pay for the welfare state. And yet the party is pledged, and rightly so, to bring taxes down. I don't see any prospect of being able to balance this part of the books by trying to spend less on welfare. After all it's still the case that we're spending much less than other countries on, for example, the modernization of our ancient hospitals or the improvement of our congested roads. How then do we square the argument? I believe that we've got to be prepared to adopt a lot of proposals that have so far been fearfully rejected: loans and not grants for university students; more realistic charges for non-vocational further education; charges for many more aspects of the health service – and for things like nursery schools; tolls for motorways – and so on. The list can be prolonged almost indefinitely; and almost every item is at the moment likely to make even a Tory politician's flesh creep. The voters, he might think, are likely to run a mile. But we have got to bring the whole issue out into the open.

'We've got to give real meaning to the other part of our traditional case – by giving people real encouragement to help themselves. This means giving them the option of spending their own money on the purchase of higher standards for themselves, outside or in addition to the state system – whether in independent schools or private medical care. And they should not, if they choose to do this, be expected to pay the whole of the cost two times over. We need to devise a fair system of tax reliefs which will save them from this. This is the way in which I believe we can, as a country, get more money coming into the improvement of the welfare state without at the same time pushing taxes through the roof. And it's a way of doing so that will enable more and more people to exercise choice in a way that is only open to a rich minority at the moment. But the argument will be a difficult one to put across unless we start discussing it openly and soon.'

In June 1970 Geoffrey Howe was re-elected to the House of Commons in a three-cornered fight with a majority of 13,029 and by happy quirk Christopher Chataway was returned even earlier at a by-election in Chichester. However, in spite of holding two government positions as Minister of Posts and Telecommunications and Minister for Industrial Development, he subsequently decided on a career in the City and left Parliament in 1974. Howe during the same Parliament was Solicitor-General and joined the Cabinet as Minister for Trade and Consumer Affairs.

Since 1970 the constituency boundaries have been redrawn to exclude Reigate and Redhill and, despite Caterham and Warlingham in the north, become a much more rural scene of some 200 square miles stretching from the borders of Greater London in the north twenty-three miles south to the edge of Sussex. To the east lies Kent. Overall the new area is still rich and prosperous with a mixture of commuter-populated villages and small towns like Oxted, Godstone and Lingfield threaded through rolling wooded countryside. While some twenty years on there is a certain interest in his role as Foreign Secretary, the problems which really trouble their green and pleasant land focus on planning and housing. Young people are frequently stymied by high prices in their hopes of home ownership, yet the comfortably and even the newly settled fight off new development which would increase the supply of new homes. Given Common Market quotas, farmers are only too anxious to find new value in their land, particularly since planning permission for housing can provide an immediate 500 per cent increase in its value. The sale of top soil and subsequent use as a rubbish tip and future rehabilitation also produces rich but equally unpopular return to the owners of farm land. Local people want the preservation of the status quo. The green belt is ever sacred, gipsies anathema, quarrying obtrusive, Gatwick a nuisance – even though large numbers of local people are dependent directly or indirectly on the airport for their work and organizations are now located in this part of England because of its convenience by motorway and airports with the rest of the country and even the world.

Sir Geoffrey has watched these changes happen and still makes a point of visiting problem sites as well as writing to local councils and fellow government ministers about his constituents' concerns. During the Vancouver Commonwealth conference in 1987 he insisted on daily storm reports following the hurricane which decimated the tree population of the south-east and left many constituents without electricity. He holds regular constituency surgeries. But as well as basking a little in the reflected glory of his high office, there is some discontent that he cannot actively campaign on their behalf. 'We believe he supports us,' says a local party member. 'But we can't really know because he can't commit himself. He has always been a minister or shadow minister and so never had the freedom of the backbench to stand up and defend our interests.'

In the early years before he became a cabinet minister, local people used to see a good deal of the Howes who rented a house locally and spent most weekends in the constituency. Nowadays he stays in Chevening which is almost on the eastern borders. Normally he manages to spend about one Friday a month in the area visiting perhaps a factory, school, shopping centre, sheltered housing, research foundation and conservation project, with lunch possibly at a local pub. There will be a brief for each visit. 'We will try to make a mix of urban and rural areas,' says Alex Finnen, his agent. 'Some are more heavily industrial and business oriented but he links in with current issues.' At the end of the afternoon, Sir Geoffrey may return to Chevening for a break and the chance to catch up on any Foreign Office matters before returning, for example, to talk to young farmers in a pub or have tea, biscuits and conversation with constituents in a local village hall. He has also run seminars for young voters and on education and health.

Because of his position in government and increasing levels of security, his entourage normally includes his driver Peter Smithson, who in past governments drove Richard Crossman; Finnen and police escorts from the Surrey constabulary as well as the Metropolitan police. In June 1987 the election convoy involved even greater levels of protection with police cars front and back with Sir Geoffrey and Lady Howe emerging from the central vehicle to cover different sides of the road. Confident, grey and portly, he would sometimes jog up to sunlit wisteria-clad cottage or council-built (if no longer council-owned) property to apologize for disturbing their afternoon and see if he could count on their vote. Each time he was escorted by at least one armed policeman while others remained on guard at garden entrances and across the road, eyes ever watchful for any danger or oddity in everyday English rural normality. The reception varied. There was the adulation: 'I've never shaken hands with a famous face before' and 'I think you've done great things for us'. There was also the man who complained about aircraft noise and lack of policing (except that afternoon) and the fact that he only received anodyne letters from government when he wrote to Sir Geoffrey. 'I do have to deal with national matters as well,' said Sir Geoffrey. The man certainly was not going to leave it at that. 'That's right,' he grumbled on. 'No good having a minister as MP.' At this point Sir Geoffrey made him shake hands.

The details of his flying canvass to selected streets in small towns and villages and a local railway station could only be known until the very last minute by the organizing party faithful. Pub lunch for a dozen could only be booked at the shortest notice and sniffer dogs checked out each of the three evening meeting village halls. Since 1983 his police escort has doubled.

'The United Kingdom is seen by economists, politicians, governments, ordinary people around the world as the success story of the 1980s,' he told one audience in Bletchingly.

81

Undoubtedly the local majority took his message to heart and rewarded him for his role in that success. Sir Geoffrey's majority in 1987 was 18,126, almost double that of 1974, when the constituency was first redrawn.

9

The Legal Alternative

Geoffrey Howe, Patrick Jenkin (his flatmate in Denning Road, Hampstead) and Bruce Griffiths got their Bar examination results on the same night in 1952. Like many students they went along late that evening to *The Times*, then still in Printing House Square at Blackfriars, to read the page proof of the first edition on a noticeboard. Their subsequent informal celebration was followed in due course by formal dinners in their respective inns, the Middle Temple in the case of Geoffrey Howe. A full white-tie occasion, the young men were summoned in turn to the bench by the Master Treasurer in traditional style: 'I call you to the Utter Bar and publish you barrister.' One of Howe's first jobs, worth two guineas, came from his father in Port Talbot. He wanted an opinion on a will and suggested that he involve Bruce Griffiths and split the fee. Howe then began to develop a general practice, most of his work relating to personal injury and factory accidents, his briefs coming from trades unions to represent employees.

His many friends at the Bar praise his advocacy. Robert Sheaf, his friend from Winchester days, who by coincidence joined the same chambers, can remember overhearing a conversation between Norman Richards QC, Howe's pupil master, and his own master about the extraordinarily high quality of his work for someone with so little experience. Now, years after he has been totally absorbed by politics, Howe is still held in high regard for his professional skill. People remember him as both strategist and tactician, for his overall judgement, ability to grasp and analyse issues, thorough preparation, concise logical summing up, his gently persuasive manner and above all his sense of fairness. As happens with many of his political speeches today, while his delivery gave the impression of stolidity, the substance was quite different. He would also give the impression, as he quietly referred to evidence and precedent, that the court had only to trust him, write down what he said and their judgement would become obvious. 'Of all the people at the Bar, he's the one I consciously think of when I'm in a hole and think how would he cope and what would he do,' says one younger QC, who worked alongside Howe for several years and has also reached the higher echelons.

As might be expected from his House of Commons performances, sensible speeches and quiet comments on radio and television, declamatory advocacy with strong emotional appeal would have been totally out of character. He was, as now, master of his brief, cool under pressure, dispassionate and intelligent. He was very much the lawyers' lawyer, of greater appeal to a judge than a jury. Indeed according to one legal friend: 'The judge would simply sit there and beam and look as if he was with him even when he didn't particularly want to be.'

Geoffrey Howe spent a good deal of time on the Wales and Chester circuit and became a Queen's Counsel at thirty-eight. To take 'silk' is a major step in any barrister's career. Every year there appears in the Court page of *The Times* a small notice to the effect that applications can now be made. At that point men and women with at least ten years' practice and sufficient confidence in their experience, ability, expertise and reputation will sound out fellow professionals about their chances of acceptance by the Lord Chancellor, who carries out his own sounding out process with a number of judges. Refusal, if not humiliating, is certainly discouraging and few try more than three times.

In practical terms the accolade of QC affects status, income and dress. A QC can attend the Lord Chancellor's annual breakfast following the special service in Westminster Abbey.

The new QC has to purchase a black silk frock coat and gown to wear in court and, although the simple barrister's wig suffices on the job, a full bottomed wig, like that of a judge, has to be bought for about £900 for ceremonial occasions. On the financial side the fees are so much higher that clients may prefer to choose a junior (in other words, an ordinary barrister who is not a QC but has similar experience). And since fees are settled by the clerk to chambers – indeed a barrister is forbidden to discuss such matters – there can be no question of taking the honour and not running the risk. To take silk therefore at thirty-eight, as did Howe, normally cautious, still with a young family and an MP of only one-year's standing in what proved to be a marginal seat, signalled courage and confidence as well as the respect of his superiors.

Geoffrey Howe's involuntary absence from the House of Commons when he lost Bebington gave him time to participate in a number of cases and inquiries with political and personal significance. At 9.15 am on 21 October 1966 disaster struck in his home country of Wales, when one of the coal tips on Merthyr Mountain slid into the valley in a most terrible black avalanche to destroy 116 children, five teachers, twenty-three other adults, and property in Aberfan. When the rush of debris came to a halt, silence cloaked the valley. 'In that silence, you could not hear a bird or a child.' a local resident told the subsequent inquiry. The country too was temporarily silenced by the horror of the tragedy, the loss of so much young life and laughter and the ease with which the potential for disaster can build up within the over-confident, everyday practice of respectable organizations. Aberfan was perhaps even more devastating than similarly terrible events since because the accident affected just one small community and so many children.

Howe was called in to represent local officials at the tribunal which sat for seventy-six days between the end of November and May 1967. His friend Bruce Griffiths was his junior. There is a natural drama in court cases or tribunals but the Aberfan inquiry had all the makings of a Greek tragedy. The fact that the National Coal Board fought to the end created additional bitterness. For Howe and Griffiths it was a difficult, challenging brief. After hearing 136 witnesses, whose evidence ran to 4,236 pages of foolscap and was probed by the Attorney General, eight QCs and eleven juniors, the tribunal, chaired by the Rt Hon Lord Justice Edmund Davies, concluded that Aberfan was 'a terrifying tale of bungling ineptitude by many men charged with tasks for which they were totally unfitted, of failure to heed clear warnings and of total lack of direction from above. Not villains, but decent men, led astray by foolishness or by ignorance or by both in combination, are responsible for what happened.'

The whole saga deeply affected Howe. In his personal capacity he found himself in the professional advocate's most fundamental role, as a buffer between the accused and the natural seekers of vengeance. In his political capacity he was staggered by the combination of power and diffuse responsibility, if not irresponsibility, in a remote nationalized monopolistic industry over which a small local council could exert little, if any, influence. He gave some indication of his concern when he spoke one year later to The Medico-Legal Society in London about one of the local men he represented and who was prepared to assume a share of the blame, unlike the NCB as a whole.

'I ask you for a moment to consider the case of one individual who was criticized by the tribunal,' Howe told the meeting. 'It was said that he "cannot be wholly absolved from a measure of blame for the disaster." He was the most junior of all the officials and was the colliery mechanical engineer. His great grandfather sank the original pit shaft of the colliery and his grandfather and father were overmen there.

'He was born in 1923 in Aberfan when the second of the mountain tips was going up. He attended the Pantglas Junior School, which was destroyed and his family and friends were scattered throughout the village. He left school at the age of fourteen to work at the coal face in 1937. He became a pipe fitter's apprentice and in due course a fitter and in 1952, with no special training, he was appointed as the "colliery mechanic" responsible for all the complicated mechanical apparatus above and below ground and for 260 men. He never received at any time in his life one word of instruction about tips or any of the technicalities, nor even a definition of his responsibility for them. No system was ever laid down for him to comply with.

'His evidence is striking. Perhaps the most striking of all was when he was asked by counsel for the tribunal about his responsibility. He was asked:

"**Q** At the time of your appointment, from that time onwards until the disaster, was there ever a discussion between you and any other senior official about the safety of Tip No. 7?
"**A** No, Sir.

"**Q** Were you ever instructed to keep a record in relation to the tips of the way in which they behaved?
"**A** No, Sir.

"Then – this, I thought was an impressive moment – he was asked:

"**Q** You regarded your appointment and your responsibilities in connection with the tips as being supervision of the mechanical apparatus and of the men and of nothing else?
"**A** Well, that would be it, Sir, yes. I had no instructions at all about any tips in writing but only the mechanical side, Sir. But I was responsible. It is no good shirking it. I was responsible for the tip."

'That required great courage in a man of that background and qualification before that tribunal at that time,' Howe continued. 'It was in this respect that he was "not wholly absolved from a measure of blame". It is interesting to consider that verdict against the wider background. The National Coal Board, at all levels, had never devised a policy for the safety of tips. The National Union of Mineworkers had never suggested one. Her Majesty's Inspectorate for Mines and Quarries had never canvassed the problem. The Mining Qualification Board and the Safety in Mines Research Advisory Board had never considered it. The Royal Commission on Safety in Coal Mines in 1938 never suggested it. Both Houses of Parliament, when they passed the Mines and Quarries Act in 1954, never canvassed the possibility.'

Howe went on: 'The very tip which slipped had been seen

87

by at least a dozen reasonably qualified officials, not only of the National Coal Board, none of whom reacted with any concern of the kind which, after the event, came to be regarded as the only possible reaction of a reasonably intelligent man . . . . More than two dozen men were exposed potentially to criticism; not that number were finally criticized. The criticism at Aberfan extended up, indeed, as high as people in the Treasury who were imposing unseen controls on the pattern of capital expenditure which affected what happened on that mountain. It ranged from that level down to the charge hand, the man whose job it was simply to get rid of the muck, as he put it, on the tip. Nowhere in that pattern could one identify the place where Harry Truman's notice was displayed, "The buck stops here". That may be the contrast between our pattern of individual professional existence and the pattern in this kind of giant organization.

'Only one question was never really asked, let alone pressed to a conclusion: whether a gigantic public corporation, overshadowing as it did in scale and resources the local authority – the Merthyr Borough Council – will not always prove to be the least sensitive and most elusive body of all to manage and, where necessary, the most difficult for society itself to discipline. It was a question which it was difficult for any of those appearing before the tribunal to ask. It lay too far on the political side of the terms of reference for the residents of Aberfan or for the tribunal itself. It was hardly likely to be asked by or on behalf of the Merthyr Borough Council or by or on behalf of any of the unions who had long argued the case for the creation of just such a pattern or organization. Nor was it likely to be asked by those who looked to the same monopolistic corporation as their sole potential employer. So the question still remains to trouble us: Quis custodiet ipsos custodes?'

An even more obviously political case followed Aberfan when, in August 1967 during the legal vacation, Howe represented a group of Enfield parents who were seeking an injunction against their local London borough's plans for creating comprehensive schools. Not long before, Howe had appeared in a television-staged court case in defence of the right to send children to private schools. While arguments in favour of such

parental choice clashed with the accepted intellectual ethos
of the day, his performance in the situation contrived for the
serious watching public was good enough to lead directly to
a real-life role fighting the power of the State. It was one of
the earliest occasions on which members of the public successfully managed to win a case against government on a point
of administrative law. Basically the action related to proposals
for the amalgamation of eight schools to create new comprehensives to comply with government policy as set out by the
then Labour Secretary of State, Anthony Crosland. The
Enfield parents and ratepayers included Ralph Harris, now
Lord Harris of High Cross and chairman of the Institute of
Economic Affairs, and Ross McWhirter, who with his twin
brother Norris produced the *Guinness Book of Records*. (Following a number of subsequent legal actions relating to the freedom of the individual, Ross was assassinated by IRA gunmen
in 1975.)

According to the law, proposals for new comprehensives
had to be published, submitted to the Secretary of State and
then wait on his approval. Enfield had revised its original proposals and been advised by the Secretary of State that they
need not publish notices. In the lower court the judge thought
the balance of convenience was in favour of proceeding with
the plan, given the imminence of the new term, even though
the law had been broken. The court of appeal thought otherwise. The advice of the Secretary of State was not law. 'This
is solely a question of law,' said Lord Denning, Master of
the Rolls. 'We are not concerned in this court with the policy
of the Secretary of State or of the education authority. Nor
have we to consider whether it is good to change from a selective system of education to a comprehensive system.' Suggestions that reversing the arrangements might cause chaos and
damage teachers, pupils and the public were not relevant. 'If
a local authority does not fulfil the requirements of the law,
this court will see that it does fulfil them,' he went on in his
judgement. 'It will not listen readily to suggestions of "chaos".
The Department of Education and the council are subject to
the rule of law and must comply with it, just like everyone
else. Even if chaos should result, still the law must be obeyed.
But I do not think chaos will result. I can well see that there

may be a considerable upset for a number of people but I think it far more important to uphold the rule of law.' Represented by Geoffrey Howe, a small band of individuals had checked the power of the State. But this was not to be the end. Enfield fought back by issuing a revised scheme within eight days of the verdict, and with the bureaucracy fighters successfully going to the court on two Saturdays that September, government was shown to be acting unlawfully three times in sixteen days.

A major victory, the Enfield case also raised Howe's legal profile. It also reinforced his political interest in education and he spoke out for a parents' charter giving parents rights to consultation, representation on school governing bodies and, most important, appeal to independent public tribunals against the decisions of local education authorities allocating children to particular schools. He also pressed for the compulsory publication by schools of a full prospectus setting out their achievements and objectives. 'If the directors of limited companies are required – for the protection of prospective investors – to publish full and accurate information about their affairs, why should schools that are often near-monopoly suppliers be expected to do less?' he asked the Penarth Parent Teachers Association in September 1969. That year he had become chairman of the governors of a Tower Hamlets comprehensive school, replacing his wife Elspeth, who had stood down to join the Inner London Education Authority. 'If those who offer package holiday trips – as well as independent school proprietors – are rightly subject to the provisions of the Trade Descriptions Act,' he went on, 'why should local education authorities be allowed to go on publishing inadequately generalised "guides" to the nature of their schools? In an age when consumer protection is rightly required in so many fields, parents should be given enough detailed and accurate information to enable them to choose between different "comprehensive" schools that aspire to excel in different specialities.' At this period, he was also pressing for more private spending on schools to raise standards and widen choice; for the introduction of vouchers which parents could use to help pay private fees if they so wished; and loans to help finance any expansion of higher education. The ideas may sound familiar now but they were treading new ground then.

Meanwhile his reputation as a lawyer prospered. In 1967, as well as Enfield, Geoffrey Howe had also appeared in the Divisional Court in a case now quite simply known as ex-parte Lain. The human story was compelling, the law exceedingly complex, involving as it did the ins and outs of compensation calculations relating to a man who had died and to whom therefore a number of future payments would no longer be made. The man in question was a policeman whom a suspect shot in the face. He later became blind and then shot himself. By then he had already received interim compensation from the Criminal Injuries Compensation Board and his widow applied for further compensation. She was awarded an equivalent amount and appealed, as was her right, for reconsideration by a panel of three people. Instead of increasing the award they reduced it to nil by taking the dead policeman's pension into account. When the case went to appeal, the court backed this decision in terms of the sums involved, which meant Howe's client lost her financial claim. However, during the hearing the Criminal Injuries Compensation Board had tried to establish that their decisions could not and should not be considered in a court of law. It was to Howe's credit that they failed to place themselves beyond the law.

Geoffrey Howe was also involved in politically sensitive cases brought against Rhodesian sanction busters. However, undoubtedly his toughest and most formative challenge came with the Ely Hospital inquiry with its appalling tangle of allegations of abuse and bad management followed by a prolonged attempt by Whitehall mandarins to prevent the publication in full of his 83,000-word report. Fearful of the impact of the truth, they wished to keep most of the findings confidential and release only an abbreviated cosmetic version. Howe was told he had been invited to produce a summary of conclusions, not a book. He insisted on the publication of all essential facts and produced a lengthy partial summary including the comment that it did not do justice to the case and referring to editorial interference. He had refused to compromise. 'He had the steel to stand up to a senior government minister,' says one legal friend. 'That required integrity and courage. Most people do not tread on the toes of those in power. The smaller man is going eventually to want their good offices.' Howe says he was able to take a much more independent stance because he had a political existence. A fellow barrister says his firmness stiffened the position of chairmen of all subsequent inquiries.

The struggle lasted some three months before surfacing one night before Richard Crossman, Secretary of State for Social Services, for decision. In *The Crossman Diaries*, he expressed his outrage at being given only two days when he could have seen and thought about the issue at any time during the previous three months. He said he felt that there was no alternative to the publication of the full unabridged report and that the department should take the credit for doing this. Otherwise Howe, 'one of the cleverest Conservative lawyers', would be entitled to talk about suppression. The report was published on 27 March 1969 together with an announcement about the proposed formation of a new independent inspectorate to check the possibility of future similar abuse. In his introduction to *Selections from the Diaries of a Cabinet Minister* (Cape, 1979), Anthony Howard described this decision to publish in full in the face of all official advice as 'perhaps the bravest political action of Crossman's career'. The same might equally be said of Howe.

What was it that Whitehall so badly wished to conceal and which two politicians (although Howe was acting in a non-partisan judicial role) felt obliged to expose? The scandal emerged in August 1967 when the *News of the World* published a story about the ill-treatment of patients including pilfering of food and clothes as well as inadequate care in an unnamed hospital. That hospital was Ely, a grim nineteenth-century building in Cardiff, formerly a poor law school and workhouse, but by then classified and used as a psychiatric hospital for subnormal and mentally ill men, women and children. The Welsh Hospital Board chose Howe, a Welsh QC, to chair the subsequent inquiry. From the start, its investigations were placed in an operational straitjacket and a formal request for a solicitor to identify potential witnesses and get the gist of their evidence, was refused.

'We experienced considerable difficulty as a result of the partially blindfold way in which the inquiry had to be conducted,' the report states. 'Without any knowledge of the matters about which any particular witness was likely to speak,

our investigation necessarily had an incoherent and disorgan-
ized quality. Our time was wasted with some of the earlier
witnesses in pursuing points which were very largely disposed
of without doubt by later witnesses (of whose evidence we
were necessarily unaware until such later witnesses had come
to give their evidence). Fresh points were raised by later witnesses which ought ideally to have been investigated with those
who had already given evidence. Not all such points were pursued since, if they had been, the inquiry threatened to become
circular, if not immortal. Most, if not all, of these difficulties
could have been avoided if a solicitor had been available, as
requested by the committee, to conduct a preliminary investigation of the possible evidence. In the absence of such a solicitor to present the evidence to the inquiry, the chairman of
the committee had necessarily to cross-examine some of the
witnesses – often upon the basis of premises which later turned
out to be false and thus in a manner which must at times
have appeared unfair.' Howe particularly disliked being forced
to combine the role of judge and prosecutor and pressed the
Government to reconsider the idea of appointing a parliamentary commissioner for such cases.

The committee sat for fifteen days towards the end of 1967
and the beginning of 1968. All meetings were private, all evidence confidential, although anyone accused of malpractice
could be present. In spite of the fact that the committee had
no power to summon witnesses and both staff and relations
of patients were afraid of possible repercussions on their careers
or treatment, fifty-two people came forward. Many patients
were seen but, because of often severe disabilities, unable to
provide much help.

Following half a million words of evidence the conclusions
about the treatment of some patients and the quality of care
within the National Health Service institution were harsh. A
young epileptic, the report said, probably was teased and
assaulted on two occasions. The word 'probably' was used
several times because the committee had not been in a position
to prove individual guilt. A middle-aged man was handled
with undue roughness, wounded in the scalp and not seen
by a doctor until the following day. An elderly patient was
struck in the face on at least one occasion, as was another

young epileptic. A difficult elderly patient was isolated for unduly long periods behind bolted doors. Once, when relatives were visiting, it seemed likely that a nurse had picked up a set of false teeth from an unmarked selection in a bowl, rinsed them and tried to slip them into the mouth of a sleeping patient. Another time, the toenails of a patient were cut clumsily and with inadvertent cruelty. In most cases, the report said, there was no malice, simply the acceptance of old-fashioned, unduly rough, custodial and undesirably low standards of nursing care.

There was virtually no training, no attempt to habit train the incontinent and even sudden death was treated casually. Medical care and record-keeping lacked energy and sophistication. Nurses ate meals and fruit intended for patients regarding them as a perk of the job. Theft probably took place on a substantial scale. (The report regretted the necessity for such generalization because it would cast a slur on some people who were entirely innocent.) It was suggested that clothes went astray. Laundry was left around wards all day, with no separation of foul and dry dirty linen. The children's villas were grossly overcrowded and appallingly ill-equipped. There were no recreational or educational facilities. Many lockers (for which there was scarcely room between beds) were without doors and all were entirely empty. When toys were provided they rarely lasted more than an hour or two. All the male wards were seriously overcrowded with patients of widely differing ages and disability. Standards were reminiscent in many ways of a past era of custodial care. When a nurse had complained about the ill-treatment of a patient, his terms of duty were so changed that he resigned. 'An atmosphere had plainly come to exist at Ely in which such well-intentioned members of the nursing staff had been persuaded that it was useless, if not hazardous, to complain,' the report commented. There was no need for Howe to set out the sad, slovenly, contemptibly inefficient and uncaring picture in any but the plainest of prose.

The conclusions were equally clear ranging from major recommendations such as the need for the hospital's reconstruction; the relief of overcrowding; the investigation of sudden death; an immediate review of the nursing establishment; the introduction of someone of outstanding talent to raise mor-

ale, standards of performance and discipline; and the appointment of younger, more knowledgeable, members to the hospital
management committee; to small but important proposals
such as the provision of sufficient tooth brushes and the proper
care of false teeth.

Ely was not the only time that Geoffrey Howe had to swim
against the tide. In 1967 when the Latey Committee published
its views on the age of majority, it contained a minority report
signed by Howe and John Stebbings, another lawyer who was
later knighted and became chairman of the Law Society. While
the report argued the case for making the eighteenth birthday
all important, these two acknowledged their position as an
'awkward squad', admitted that 'a gently diffident note of
reservation' would have been much less arduous and then set
out eighty-one paragraphs of fundamental differences between
themselves and the rest of the committee. In a sense they said
that the whole business was a put-up job, that there was neither
the demand nor the need for change and indeed an opinion
poll had shown that the majority of young people aged between
sixteen and twenty-four thought that twenty-one was the right
age for responsibility with regard to marriage without parental
permission, the sale of a house and the ability to sign hire
purchase agreements. 'There are no doubt some issues on
which reformers may be justified in pressing ahead in face
of opposition from a substantial popular majority,' they wrote.
'The abolition of capital punishment was, for some of us at
least, an obvious example. But it is hard to see any reason
why teenagers should be dragged kicking and screaming into
the permissive atmosphere of the twenty-first century, if they
have no burning desire to come along.' Even if teenagers were
better off than those of a preceding generation, it did not follow
that the money which was burning a hole in their pockets
should be allowed to do so with greater ease.

While it was true that young people matured physically
at an earlier age, they went on, there was no such certainty
that they were any more psychologically mature than their
predecessors. In addition the breathing space between school
and the altar was becoming perilously narrow. At one time,
after leaving school, young people had enjoyed seven years
between fourteen and twenty-one when they were neither adult

nor children. If the age of majority was reduced to eighteen, this period would be reduced to only two years. The prolongation of full-time education – by statute and by choice – was postponing the age at which children began acquiring experience outside the classroom and was a powerful reason for maintaining the present position. In the Swinging Sixties, such doubts about the wisdom of youth must have seemed positively pedantic.

Howe also found time for membership of the Street Committee dealing in detail with legislation concerning racial discrimination and the Cripps Committee, set up by Edward Heath, the Conservative Party leader, which published a report called *Fair Share for the Fair Sex*. It covered a number of areas of discrimination and pressed for changes in the tax treatment of married women, the use of the electoral roll instead of property qualification as the basis of jury service and the abolition by the courts of consideration of a woman's possible prospects of remarriage in assessment of damages. With one other member of the committee, Beryl Cooper, he went on to write a Bow Group pamphlet on a number of other aspects of equal opportunities. There was also a legal report on the administration of the courts published under the auspices of the Society of Conservative Lawyers. 'Confidence in the fairness, integrity and independence of our legal system remains high. It is fundamental to the survival of a free society,' the introduction began quietly. 'One must acknowledge that distance lends enchantment to this view. The ordinary citizen who is brought into contact with the law is very often made uncomfortably aware of substantial defects in the day-to-day working of the system. The hearing of his case can sometimes be long delayed. When finally it does come on for trial he may be lucky to get as much as twenty-four hours' notice of what is, for him, a vitally important date. The counsel originally selected to represent him may not be available in the event. Despite the shortness of notice, he may find himself obliged to wait for hours, or even days, in the draughty passageways of a building that is ancient and ill-designed.' By the time Howe's latest contribution to reform was published in 1970, the author was once again a Member of Parliament. He was also a knight. The telephone call from Edward Heath, the new prime minister, came when he was already back on the legal circuit at the Newport assizes following the General Election. Judge Griffiths remembers he was called out, returned bubbling with exicitement and, when the court rose about a quarter of an hour later, simply had to let out the good news, strictly a secret, to one of his oldest friends. Not only was he going to be Solicitor-General but he would be handling the contentious industrial relations and Common Market legislation and therefore remain in mainstream politics. Bruce Griffiths knew that Geoffrey Howe usually called Mr Heath 'Ted' and asked what he had called him in such a momentous conversation. 'Prime Minister,' came the answer. 'I wasn't going to risk it.' However, while he wanted to make sure that the acceptance of a knighthood would not bar his further advance in the wider sphere of politics, his mother was quite simply delighted. 'Elspeth will be Lady Howe,' she said. The boy from Port Talbot was making the grade. Sadly his father, Eddie Howe, had died in 1958 and never knew about his son's political success. Meanwhile a legal friend says: 'He would have undoubtedly made an absolute fortune if he had stayed at the bar and not gone into politics.'

10

Constitutional Change

The bright hopes of June 1970 offered no clues to the ignominious manner in which Edward Heath would leave Downing Street in February 1974. The Conservatives were pledged to what Heath called 'The Quiet Revolution'.

'We will have to embark on a change so radical, a revolution so quiet and yet so total, that it will go far beyond the programme for a Parliament ... we were returned to office to change the course and history of this nation, nothing else.'

Geoffrey Howe at forty-three was one of the youngest members of the new Ministerial team. A cabinet colleague of that time comments: 'We had a memory of Geoffrey Howe as a conscientious and dutiful backbencher. He was always obedient to the whip, but we were all a little startled at Ted's choice. Ted values competent staff work and Geoffrey Howe is a first class paper-chaser as well as a good lawyer.' In Opposition in 1966 when he had last been in the Commons he had been a frontbench spokesman on labour and social services.

The objectives of the new government, as defined in the Queen's speech in July, included the reform of trade union law, integration of welfare with taxation, reduction of inflation and reduction of the state control of the economy. The speech also listed new incentives for savings and control of immigration, both of which had been regarded as potent vote winners.

Most of this programme was to fail substantively, part in a humiliating manner, part lost in the inchoate condition in which the Government came to an end. The only real legislative memorial that endures from the 1970–74 ministry was the accession to the European Economic Community. Given little prominence in the election, membership did not feature high on the agenda, even though dear to Ted Heath's heart and to his new Solicitor-General.

In his October budget the Chancellor of the Exchequer, Anthony Barber, cut 6d (2.5p) off income tax and cut corporation tax by two and a half per cent, which was balanced by the introduction of charges for some social services and cuts in others. Margaret Thatcher, the new Education Minister, made her first impact in the public arena by introducing higher charges for school meals and abolishing free school milk to cries of outrage of 'Margaret Thatcher, milk snatcher'. The Industrial Reorganization Corporation and the Prices and Incomes Board were abolished but these two corporatist ghosts were reanimated by 1974 and came to haunt the Government.

Geoffrey Howe was to have a role far more central to the performance of a government than is normally expected of the second law officer of the Crown. He was the prime political force and certainly the crucial legal force in the attempt to tame the unions. He was to rewrite the English Constitution for the first time for nine hundred years by ceding, with Parliamentary backing, the supremacy of English Law to a transnational authority through his remarkably concise ten clause Bill signifying membership of the EEC. He was also the joint architect of the attempt to control the surge of inflation by quasi-legal controls on prices when he was transmuted into Britain's first Consumer Affairs Minister.

The years 1970–74 lifted Geoffrey Howe from the second division to the first division of politics.

Apart from tax reform, no subject had exercised Ted Heath's team so much as the future of the trade unions. Everyone agreed that they were the greatest handicap to commercial prosperity. They had also become so powerful that they had become an obstacle outside the normal democratic process.

There seems to have been an age element in the willingness of the new government to implement the necessary reforms.

Older hands doubted if it was practical politics to bring the unions within the normal laws of contract. Their immunities, argued the men who remembered the 1920s and 1930s, would be fought for so tenaciously that it was better to reach some accommodation with the more moderate union bosses. But the younger men – including both Heath and Howe – were determined to bring these obdurate and obsolete bodies within the law.

On 3 December the Industrial Relations Bill was published. Nearly twenty years later its proposals seem unremarkable. However, at the time, although the Tories had talked openly of tackling trade unions in their electoral campaign, they seemed very bold. The unions and the Labour Party dedicated themselves to blocking change.

The Bill proposed to make agreements between employers and unions enforceable at law, in other words, contractual, unless, and this was an astonishing exception, the parties agreed they were not to be. Despite this huge open window preserving their rights to remain outside the law the unions regarded the Industrial Relations Bill as a death-trap.

In addition, there were to be a series of 'unfair industrial practices', breach of which would make unions liable to forfeit legal immunity. There was to be a National Industrial Relations Court as a new division of the High Court, to try cases arising from the Act. This Court was also to be given power to impose a sixty-day 'cooling-off period' if it found that a prospective strike was against the national interest. Secret ballots of union membership could be ordered by the court. The closed shop was nominally to be banned and replaced by an agency shop which dissenting workers would be forced to join if a majority of their fellow employees so voted. The Act added provisions to protect workers from unfair dismissal and imposed obligatory periods of notice for long-service employees.

Although the Department of Employment was led by Robert Carr, the Solicitor-General held the reins of leadership with respect to this all-important innovation.

Shortly before his death in 1987, Stephen Abbot, Geoffrey Howe's special adviser at the time, said: 'Ted Heath trusted and liked Robert Carr, but Geoffrey always knew exactly what was needed. Carr played at being emollient, but Geoffrey's calm ponderous style hid from no one that he was out for the trade unions' balls.'

Howe, said Abbot, took the Department of Employment by storm. Ministry officials had come to accept over the years that its cultural role was to work with the unions, either out of sympathy or fear.

'No one thought we could actually beat them. Our arrival was a shock. They thought they were the experts on trade union law but Geoffrey Howe demonstrated he not only knew as much but he could see better alternatives. He gained the initiative in the Department. Robert Carr seemed content,' said Abbot.

In the Commons, Howe's understanding of the law and foreign industrial relations practices was so obviously assured and confident that the House came to accept that the Bill was the Solicitor-General's and not the Employment Secretary's. Howe assiduously wrote articles and spoke publicly around the country explaining the Bill's virtues. Vic Feather of the TUC said: 'Geoffrey Howe may try to defeat us by tedium, but he will not mesmerise us into oblivion'.

Howe enjoyed the opportunity to address the London meeting of the American Bar Association just before his Bill was passed. The changes he envisaged would 'take place not in response to the will of one particular government but in response to a widely shared sense of national need. The democratic will for change, the desire for an orderly and effective framework of law has been taking shape throughout the last decade. This is why we can be confident that the substance of our new law is likely to endure.'

Howe delighted in referring to a text from Sidney Webb, a father figure of British Socialism, expressing the view: 'I cannot believe that a civilized community will permanently continue to abandon the adjustment of industrial disputes – and, incidentally, the conditions of life of the mass of its people – to what is, in reality, the arbitrament of private war.'

Geoffrey Howe told audiences that the bitter hostility to the Act was understandable, even welcome, in so far as it let opponents express their fears. He knew he had no intention of killing off the unions, even if they would not believe this.

Although many elements in the Act were not unlike the legislation abandoned by the Wilson Government, the Labour Party committed its energies to defeating the Bill in Parliament. This was the most bitterly contested piece of legislation of the Heath Government. Ceding British sovereignty to the EEC went through quietly in comparison to the all-night sittings, filibustering and clause skirmishing. Geoffrey Howe's quiet, unemotional manner might cool some of the passions but it did not prevent a heated battle. The Bill absorbed 450 hours of parliamentary time and its Royal assent in August 1971 marked only the beginning of hostilities.

The unions' vehement antagonism included a determination to defy the law which, according to Stephen Abbot, startled Howe and Carr. They had expected the parliamentary process and the sheer reasonableness of the reforms to blunt opposition once the Bill had gone through.

The first practical challenge came in 1972 in the docks where the arrival of container technology was eroding jobs and old labour practices. The dockers – members of the country's largest union, the Transport and General Workers – objected to the loading of containers by non-dockers. The companies involved in shipping goods were equally delighted at the opportunity to find an alternative labour supply without costly out-of-date work practices and demarcation boundaries. In London, Liverpool and Hull the TGWU blacked lorries carrying containers. The firms affected asked the new National Industrial Relations Court to test the legality of the union's action and the union, found guilty of unfair industrial practice, was told to lift the blacking.

But the blacking continued. On 29 March 1972, Sir John Donaldson, President of the Court, fined the TGWU £5,000 for disregarding the court order. This figure was raised to £50,000 for contempt after the union had 'advised' its local shop stewards to comply – and they refused. Donaldson ruled that the defiance of union officers was not a defence and that local shop stewards should be disciplined or removed from office. On 13 June the union's arguments in the Appeal Court were upheld and previous rulings and fines were quashed. The certainty and clarity of the new law, which were meant to be its primary virtue, were compromised. By the end of July

the House of Lords had resolved the confusion by upholding
Sir John Donaldson's original ruling. But by then it was too
late.

For during the interval, when the Court of Appeal's mistaken
ruling was in force, three different TGWU dockers, who were
blacking a London transport firm, refused to appear before
or accept the ruling of the Industrial Relations Court. Sir John
Donaldson protested: 'By their conduct these men are saying
that they are above the law. No court should ignore such a
challenge. To do so would imperil all law and order.' On 16
June 30,000 dockers were on strike in solidarity with the three
men who continued their picketing role. They were obviously
hoping to be arrested and to enjoy the fame of martyrs. Indeed
the entire union movement was spoiling for a fight. But they
were saved from this destiny and the Government from humi-
liation by the emergence of the Official Solicitor from obscurity
to apply to the High Court for the IRC's order to be quashed.
Under long standing legislation all cases, in which people are
imprisoned for contempt of court, are reviewed by this office
and it emerged that there had been defects in the complex
administrative procedure. The Government had been saved
from a total clash with British trade unionism. Yet what looked
like a tactical victory served to rob the new Industrial Relations
Act of momentum. The Conservatives may have been very
well prepared in terms of the technical details of their reform,
but they did not have, at that time, the will to fight a bitter
and protracted war with theTUC and Labour Party. The promise behind the Bill had been industrial reconciliation and
peaceable settlement of disputes. However, if the labour movement was willing to accept jail sentences and create more
damaging strikes, that promise had evaporated.

The railway workers were the next to challenge the Act
and win. The National Union of Railwaymen ordered a work-
to-rule by its 200,000 members in support of a sixteen per
cent play claim. The Government applied for the statutory
cooling-off period, and the NUR complied. However, without
any subsequent agreement between union and management
the work-to-rule was resumed. On 13 May the Government,
having argued that ordinary railwaymen did not support the
militants and were intimidated by hand votes, used its powers

to force a secret ballot. The Government and the Tory Party at large were discredited when the ballot revealed a six to one vote in support of the NUR leadership.

Geoffrey Howe told a Conservative meeting in Oxted that: 'Industrial relations in Britain did not turn sour overnight. They have been drifting into deeper and deeper disorder for at least a quarter of a century. The process of reform will be long and difficult.'

He acknowledged that the Act was seen to be crumbling but went on: 'We should all be well advised to treat industrial relations, which after all concern relationships between human beings as a "No Crow Area". We should resist the temptation to treat the court proceedings as though it were some kind of sporting contest, with the football swinging from end to end of the field.'

Yet he was so hard pressed in his search for comfort he had to tell his audience that 1,600 new claims for unfair dismissal under the Act were proof of its success.

The Government hit another round of trouble when five dockers were jailed in July for opposing container developments. Again the Official Solicitor found procedural defects and the Court of Appeal released the prisoners. But ministers, including the Solicitor-General, had not wanted to see a national dock strike with dockers in jail.

With the dissolution of the coherence of the Industrial Relations Act the Selsdon phase of Ted Heath's Government had petered out. The remaining years were characterized by ever higher public spending in the hope of mitigating unemployment and appeasing the trade union interest.

In November 1972, Rolls Royce, a British company with a world-wide reputation, ran into imminent bankruptcy. The Government, unwilling to see the firm liquidated, announced its nationalization although receivership might have kept the firm going, as might abandonment of the crushing expense of the RB2-11 aero-engine. To the Labour Party's understandable glee, the Government adopted a Socialist response.

References to the rule of law and the need to reform trade unions melted away from the Solicitor-General's texts, as they did from those of all ministers. Informally and discreetly the kaleidoscope of policy had moved on to national incomes policies. Perhaps the industrial relations legislation repealed by the Labour Government after the 1974 election, had gone too far, too early. Nevertheless, the industrial relations court survived as the employment appeals tribunal. Since then the rest has been resurrected on a more gradual basis during a period when the unions have lost considerable influence, power and membership.

Legislation to enable Britain's entry into Europe was, of course, the Solicitor-General's other main preoccupation during this period. Geoffrey Howe had been convinced during his Bow Group days that Britain ought to be in the Common Market. However, most Conservatives were lukewarm or indifferent and official enthusiasm for the EEC was aided and abetted by the heavy knuckle-duster tactics employed by Ted Heath's whips to crush incipient opposition. Most Euro-advocates, who professed the depth of their convictions, had largely ignored the subject in election addresses and even the party manifesto had only talked about negotiation. However, while many politicians were bored or browbeaten into submission, Geoffrey Howe, at least, was pursuing a policy to which he was dedicated in heart and mind.

The treaty promised to be one of the most elaborate pieces of legislation ever presented to Parliament. No nation had then joined the European Economic Community after its institutions had been formed and the legal and technical problems looked enormous. The philosophical and even practical implications are still being discovered.

Geoffrey Howe was exhilarated by Europe. He envisaged a re-invigoration of British industry, a more assured food source, a liberalization of people's attitudes and a bulwark for peace. Just on twenty years later, while some of these aims are being fulfilled, the subsidy machine which is the Commission has lost any glamour and political lustre in the swollen budget demands and surpluses of the Common Agricultural Policy.

Howe regretted that so few of his fellow citizens, or even MPs, shared his vision: 'The great European debate is one of the manifestations of a divide in our society,' he told the Institute of Public Relations in April 1973 after British entry. 'Of course there was room – there still is room – for deep arguments about our accession to the European Community. But for too many people (on both sides) the debate never began. Or if it did, it began and ended on the wrong premises or upon premises that were totally misunderstood. Too many people thought that we were seeking to enter Europe because we wanted to be chasing after some imagined tradition that had been compounded by the Vandals in conspiracy with the Vatican. I dare say that some people too were easily persuaded that the Treaty of Rome was an instant, fail-safe, prescription for pan-European Periclean democracy. Most of the time we kept our feet more firmly on the ground.

'We knew, and still know, that we were embarking upon a long haul towards the creation of a European society that could enable us to overcome the divisiveness of nationalism without destroying patriotism.

'Of course it will be hard work. But for us the butter mountains of Brussels are not, as our critics suggest, a monumental demonstration of the inescapable folly of the entire enterprise. Rather it is evidence of the difficulty of devising a system in which the farmer and the consumer can both enjoy a decent living.'

As it is, the years which saw British, Irish and Danish admission, followed by Greece, Portugal and Spain seem to have driven farmers and consumers further apart, although it should be said that subventions for agriculture continue to disfigure not just the European market but the entire world food system.

For fifty-three days of debate Parliament was absorbed in the European Communities Bill. Two million words were uttered in the Commons, and a further half million in the Lords. Howe reckoned he was on duty in the House for 325 hours as the Bill progressed. He spoke on ninety-one occasions. His special interest was the law. It needed the most infinite of detailed knowledge and painstaking, unflappable style to convince critics that Britain's independence was not being surrendered. In an area that naturally provoked jealousies and with the whips using all their powers to browbeat dissent, Howe's complete absence of malice and his sincerity of purpose was a Parliamentary asset.

He explained that the purpose of the original Treaties of Paris and Rome was to establish a 'Common Market' and that instead of just relaxing and then abolishing tariff barriers to trade, uniform rules had to be imposed throughout the area of the market. As these rules must be impartial, they had to be above national discretion. He envisaged the powers of the Community law as limited to economic transactions. He felt the English and Scottish legal systems would remain intact and that common law would remain the basis of British courts even if the EEC Act acknowledged the unreserved supremacy of the Community law. Community regulations would be binding on British Departments of State and on the courts, as they would in other member states.

Although Geoffrey Howe has long since abandoned his former discipleship of Enoch Powell, mainly over racial issues but also over Europe, he very much respects his former mentor's intellect and logic. During the run-up to the European legislation he re-read Powell's arguments questioning the whole legitimacy of European entry. Although convinced that the Tory Party had a broad-brush mandate, the Solicitor-General was not so sure that the issue of supremacy had been fully explained or understood by the British people. Legal complexities were such that few people ever got to grips with the constitutional implications. However, he decided then, and firmly believes now that the electorate had endorsed the principle of Community membership and thus the concept of the supremacy of Community law, which went with it. Certainly he feels the matter was set beyond doubt by the Wilson Government referendum in 1975.

For the record, it is worth looking at Clause 2 of the European Communities Act which has subordinated to Community law Parliament's laws and previous court interpretations: 'All such rights, powers, liabilities, obligations and restrictions from time to time created or arising by or under the treaties, and all such remedies and procedures from time to time provided for by or under the treaties, as in accordance with the treaties, are without further enactment to be given legal effect or used in the United Kingdom, shall be recognized and available in law, and be enforced, allowed and followed accordingly; and the expression "enforceable Community right" and similar expressions shall be read as referring to one to which this subsection applies.'

Even admirers thought there was an element of sleight of hand in achieving so much by so little, but Howe says it was all devised at the time of Lord Gardiner, the Labour Lord Chancellor. However, membership of the EEC involves the transfer of legislative and judicial powers to Community institutions and a corresponding limitation of the exercise of national powers in those fields. But then membership of any organization requires a certain amount of give and take.

Professor JDB Mitchell, a professor of law at Edinburgh University and an august critic of the Bill, offered his verdict at the time: 'From a legal point of view, the Bill is good. Indeed the draftsmen should be congratulated on producing an artistic piece of legislation which ingeniously achieves the desired results and avoids betraying any of the essential characteristics of Community law. Thus the Government has demonstrated proper loyalty to the Communities.'

All UK legislation and common law conventions were to be superseded and rendered ineffective by controlling and limiting the way in which courts could act. There was even a question as to whether or not Parliament could repeal the European Communities Act and whether or not Parliament could pass future legislation which by design or accident conflicted with Community law. Geoffrey Howe formally advised Parliament in the course of one of the debates that, if a subsequent Act of Parliament were expressly to make provision 'notwithstanding Section 2 of the European Communities Act, 1971', then the Bill, to the extent so specified, could be repealed, but that, while his country was deemed a constituent state of the EEC, individual laws could not over-ride the European law. 'The creation of the European Community is one of the most exciting seminal things which has happened,' he says today. 'You cannot achieve that without breaking or making new legal instruments.'

Howe acknowledges that the Parliamentary draftsmen, led by Sir John Fiennes, excelled themselves in the design of the Act, but his own contribution was enormous. Both Lord Hailsham, the then Lord Chancellor, and Sir Peter Rawlinson, the Attorney General, expressed their admiration for the elegance and simplicity of Howe's solution to a possible legal nightmare. Edward Heath was grateful for the more than workmanlike performance of the Welsh barrister he had called out of a South Wales court little more than two years before.

11

The Heath Débâcle

In November 1972 Geoffrey Howe was offered the new role of Trade and Consumer Affairs Minister. Ted Heath gave Peter Walker, the Secretary of State for Trade and Industry, a choice: Margaret Thatcher or Geoffrey Howe. He chose the Solicitor-General. This time the telephone call caught him at Swinton College in Yorkshire, the now defunct Tory Party staff college, where he was defending his trade union reforms to an assorted audience of Tory activists.

The new ministry was a policy turnround for Heath who had scrapped the Labour-created Consumers Council in the first months of the Government. For Howe the appointment placed him another rung up the political ladder, took him into the Cabinet for the first time (although unusually at his former salary) and distanced him from the trade union battles. It also placed him at the centre of the economics debate administering the Government's new controls on prices and incomes.

Howe described his new job as having two purposes: 'One is to step up competition in many parts of our national life and the second is to give better protection to the consumer against things that operate unfairly at the moment.' He sought to widen the powers of the Restrictive Practices Court to tackle services as well as goods.

But the Government's fear of further offending the unions

was confirmed when he acknowledged that their restrictive practices would not be tackled. 'The Monopolies Commission will be able to investigate the operation of restrictive practices in industry but only with a view to setting out the facts about those matters and making recommendations. It will have no power to back up its reports with any order or the enforcement of anything at all.' The brave talk of June 1970 and the application of common law principles to unions had apparently gone.

He set up a new quango, the Office of Fair Trading which drew its powers from the 100-page Fair Trading Bill and provided the essential framework for today's monopolies and mergers legislation and the enforcement of competition. Although the middle-class professions, including his own, which have long operated restrictive practices in some cases as elaborate and costly as the blue-collar trades, had been excluded from the restrictive practices court, they were exposed for the first time to the Monopolies Commission. Since then a number of reports have led for example to the removal of bans on advertizing by the professions, the loss by solicitors of their established monopoly on conveyancing and changes in former Stock Exchange demarcation between jobbers and brokers resulting in the Big Bang and the explosion of financial markets and the importance of the City of London as a world centre.

Howe said of the role in a Conservative Political Centre pamphlet published at the time: 'A minister for consumer affairs, I soon discovered, has to act as a kind of political lightning conductor. Consumerism is, in a sense, rather like a series of electric storms. Sudden flashes of light illuminate the market in which we all live as consumers and producers together. Sometimes, but not often, the illuminations take the form of sheet lightning. Upon these occasions one is able to see not only the problem but also the solution at one and the same time. But often, much more often, I become the political conductor of a single angry flash of forked lightning. The problem is immediately clear, but the solution far from clear.'

While in the Department of Trade and Industry, Geoffrey Howe also introduced the Supply of Goods (Implied Terms) Act and the Insurance Companies Amendment Act, which were devised to clarify contract law in favour of customers. Otherwise the office focus concerned projects to improve arbitration procedures for consumers, the creation of a network of consumer advice centres and increased representation of consumers on nationalized industries and in the EEC.

After the intellectual challenge of the European Communities legislation and the sheer endurance involved in dealing with industrial relations, the Minister for Trade and Consumer Affairs was less in the limelight but well placed to enhance his experience and pick up credentials. Even today he remains a Vice-President of the Consumers Association, the voluntary wing of the consumers movement, described by Howe as 'men and women in a bargain-hunting, handbag at the ready, kind of mood ... citizens who require goods and services ... and who ought to have choices.'

In some ways his transfer from the high drama of industrial relations and the European Treaty to a world of Citizen's Advice Bureaux and local authority trading standards officers may have seemed comparatively tame. As a member of his private office in the Department of Trade commented: 'We all thought consumerism was cosmetic stuff with little content. It all seemed cotton wool. The Office of Fair Trading was called the Office of Candy Floss at the Department in Victoria Street.'

However, there was an aspect to his brief which, although very much flowing with the philosophy and ideology of the times, must have stretched the well thought out principles and policies of a man who fundamentally believes and believed in the virtues of a market economy. The very day he was appointed to the job, the Government announced legal controls on wages and prices, which was eventually to leave Britain with no better balance between full employment, union power and inflation than had the ill-fated Industrial Relations Act. Although Sir Geoffrey stoutly defends the attempt and his unexecuted plans for return to free bargaining and the market, friends say that, even with his entrée to the Cabinet, it was not a happy period. Howe remembers Ted Heath saying: 'This time we are going to sail through the whirlpool' and is loyal enough to add today: 'If anyone was ever going to make a go of that kind of approach, it would have been Ted.' But it took all his tact when as Chancellor, ten years later to the day, he met up with his French opposite number, who was in the process of imposing strict controls. Howe gently emphasized the long-term need for their removal.

The acceptance by the Minister for Trade and Consumer Affairs that he should actively participate in a political venture that was to prove so futile and thankless raises some question about the consistency of his allegiance to a liberal and open society. Sir Geoffrey disputes that price controls are incompatible with the rule of law, but he has since conceded that they are useless to defeat inflation. But then it needs to be said that, apart from Nicholas Ridley, who lost office immediately, no other member of the Government dissented from the 180 degree reversal of policy and philosophy. Prices and incomes control, which now seems so misguided, had been called for at the 1982 Tory Party conference and was backed by the majority if not altogether wholeheartedly by some. Like the rest of his fellow ministers at the time, Howe seems to have been so absorbed in the day-to-day tasks of office that he never lifted his eyes to see he was patiently helping to build a more state-controlled economy. Friendly critics say he is by nature such a team player and so loyal to his colleagues that it would never have occurred to him to resign and, if it had entered his mind, he would have thought it imprudent to dissent. But one free market exponent remembers telling Geoffrey Howe that he was being detached from his roots, that wages control had never worked and would not work this time and that he was being made the super instrument of Heath's folly. Howe was obviously uncomfortable in the role but had decided that it was better to remain in the driving seat and try to steer a more moderate course.

The idea of a 'National Dividend', to be agreed by Government, TUC, and CBI and derided by the Tories before 1970, was incorporated in the counter-inflation legislation. Labour MP Richard Crossman said that the Department of Trade's promotion of prices and incomes policies, consumer para-state bodies and the Industrial Development Executive with its regional subsidies and enforced monopolies only demonstrated that the civil service machine had captured Tory ministers. With very few independent policy sources outside Whitehall and a Tory party conditioned to uncritical obedience, it was difficult for ministers to resist the calm glaciers of departmental advice to return to interventionism.

Returning to Cambridge to speak to Conservative students in November 1972 Howe said: 'What we can, and are determined to do, is to hold back our rate of inflation. Even in relation to food prices our policy is intended to hold back the pressure towards rising prices. We have had the greatest co-operation from the Retail Consortium, from the food manufacturers and indeed from the great majority of retailers. In particular, they should not be increasing their cash margins, still less are they entitled to increase profits. The Government will rigorously scrutinize any cases where it appears wholesalers or retailers are seeking to go beyond their previous cash margins. This strict scrutiny applies to food as well as any other commodity.'

Howe's abandonment of his liberal ideals reached a low point in his praise of the mirage of price controls. While the Treasury was busy diluting the currency, the real source of price increases, he told audiences: 'The Government's prices units are playing an important part. In my department, Trade and Industry, we have now dealt with 20,000 calls ... enquiries about the mechanics of the freeze ... Our activity has had a notable influence. Price increases over the last three weeks since the standstill policy came into force have been severely moderated and a number of prices which are raised after 6th November have been put back to pre-November levels. I am glad to say Woolworth's have decided to withdraw price increases in all their 1,084 branches. Similarly Airfix, the toy manufacturers, have withdrawn price increases which were to have come into force this month. Another example where a firm has agreed to call off a price increase is British Cellophane, a subsidiary of Courtaulds ... The Government is taking a tough line. This is what the public wants. Supported by public opinion, we intend to go on fighting to keep prices down.'

Like most Conservative audiences, the Cambridge students were respectful and only a few voices queried what prices were for if not to express values and costs and that the eroding value of the pound was a disease of money, not a sign of grocer's or wholesaler's misanthropy. The veiled menacing talk of 'appropriate government action' against people who increased their prices sounds mild. But it was the authentic voice of corporatist authoritarianism.

In the period between 1972 and 1974 the Heath Government nationalized Rolls-Royce, directed industry, set prices, controlled imports and spent far beyond its revenue. By 1973 the state was controlling 60 per cent of gross domestic product. Even Keynes had thought 25 per cent high. Joy on the Labour benches was not mirrored by any public doubts by the rising men of the Tory Party. However, politics is a collective and collegial game. It is very difficult for ministers to criticize the party and government for which they have worked and struggled.

On 1 January 1973 the United Kingdom formally became a member of the EEC but all efforts to celebrate what Ted Heath and his two main European aides, Geoffrey Rippon and Geoffrey Howe, had achieved failed to inspire or provoke popular interest. Everyone was too preoccupied by the fight against inflation, which accelerated later that year when the war between Israel and the Arab states led to cuts in oil production and further price rises. In the Department of Employment the inflation-fighting team announced that pay rises would be limited to seven per cent or £2.25p a week. Threshold payments of 40p a week were permitted if the Retail Price Index rose by seven per cent. More would be allowed for those working 'unsocial' hours.

Although this formula had been devised between the Department of Employment and Joe Gormley of the National Union of Mineworkers, when the National Coal Board offered the miners thirteen per cent in October, the union chose to ban overtime. Pit production fell as winter approached. On 13 November a state of emergency was declared again and restrictions were placed on the use of electricity. Heath and his colleagues told meetings around the country that Gormley was defying not simply the Coal Board but the Government and the Government was expressing the view of the country. If that was so, said Joe Gormley, they should go to the country and hold an election. He was confident that a Labour Party, dedicated to extinguishing Geoffrey Howe's Industrial Relations Act, would win. The Labour Party had also promised to renegotiate the terms of the treaty of accession to the EEC and offer the British people a referendum to decide whether their future would lie within or without Europe.

By December industry in Britain was on a three-day week. Ted Heath said he could entertain no more concessions to the miners and on 7 February 1974 he called an election on the theme of Who Governs Britain?

Geoffrey Howe sent a message to his constituents in East Surrey to say that no one had worked harder to 'secure support and understanding for our pay and prices policies. We have spent days discussing our approach with trade union leaders and in taking account of all they had to say. It has been a privilege for me to witness the patience, the moderation and determination with which the Prime Minister has led the long series of talks at Chequers and Number 10 ... In a world of soaring prices it is impossible to freeze shop prices for more than a brief time ... If world inflation is battering our prosperity, then all the more reason why we should defend ourselves from home-grown, wage-fed inflation.'

Throughout January, as the Government seemed set on an election, Geoffrey Howe made speeches and issued a burst of press releases under the banner of Downing Street, the DTI, Central Office and his constituency. They stressed that an incomes policy was not meant to be divisive, that it had been designed to mollify the unions. A tone of exasperation creeps into his normally placid prose. It did indeed seem perverse of the NUM, having won so much from the state, still to want free collective bargaining.

For the election Geoffrey Howe concentrated on Surrey. The constituency had of course been changed and residents in the more rural commuter territory east of Reigate were told that a determined incomes policy was essential for prosperity and the defeat of inflation. Like the rest of the country it seemed true the first week, but hollow by the third. The Tories won 200,000 more votes nationwide than Labour but fewer seats. Mr Heath, after failing to find a lifeline from the Liberals, resigned.

Lord Joseph has explained the myopia which induced the Tories placid acceptance of a full-bodied Socialist programme by the fact that everyone was thoroughly absorbed by their departmental briefs. That may mitigate criticism, and of course hindsight more than helps clarify vision, but the Department of Trade and Industry was at the heart of the high-spending and price-controlling initiatives. Geoffrey Howe was in the cockpit of government and his association with these failed policies and the Industrial Relations Act could all too easily have permanently tarnished his reputation.

For, if Geoffrey Howe, unlike Margaret Thatcher and Sir Keith Joseph, has never publicly repudiated this unhappy period, he was one of if not the first Tory minister to use time in Opposition to search out and assess new ways of tackling old problems, expound proposed changes in policy and then put them into practice as Chancellor of the Exchequer. In that role, he not only refused to entertain the folly of quasi-legal price controls but showed he understood that inflation's source is found in the print rooms of the Treasury and the Bank of England, in other words in money supply. As Chancellor he was also prepared to see unemployment rise and an over-manned, underproductive British economy was forced at last to face up to the competitive pressures of the modern world. He had learnt from his experience of events and actions as a junior departmental and Cabinet minister and was tough enough to withstand the opprobrium when he later laid the economic foundations for radical change.

Meanwhile the electorate had ended the second most evangelical Socialist ministry Britain has experienced. Only the 1945 Attlee Government had been so faithful to ideas of central control and direction. It was curious that it was to be the trade unions which humbled an administration which so faithfully served them. As the Labour Party took over, its leader Harold Wilson offered the formula of social contracts, which led the way back to more open markets, and the new Chancellor of the Exchequer, Denis Healey, was to give unsung birth to monetarism. But such are the quirks of history.

12

In Opposition

The removal vans taking Mr Heath's grand piano and furniture away from Downing Street marked the last episode of an unhappy period. Geoffrey Howe, like most of the Conservative Party, said nothing for several weeks. Although he had held East Surrey with ease, the future looked bleak. The Labour Party had only a tenuous majority and it seemed likely that Harold Wilson, the new Prime Minister, would contrive to boost the economy, accommodate the unions and then seek a clear Parliamentary mandate leaving the Tories to serve on the Opposition benches for several years to come.

The former Trade and Consumer Affairs Minister first spoke in April, eight weeks after the defeat. He was uncharacteristically sarcastic about the trade unions and the dispensations being offered by the new Employment Secretary, Michael Foot: 'Few people,' he said 'can argue that Britain's trade union bosses are amongst the most gravely oppressed or underprivileged citizens in our community. Why then Mr Foot's current preoccupations? With as much frenzy as if he were answering a Mayday emergency call, he is hastening, not simply to restore but substantially to extend, the rights and privileges accorded to trade unions before 1971. Where, for example, is the sense in the proposed extension of the rights of pickets, or where is the sense in the proposal to extend the immunity of trade unions from any kind of action in any court of law? Trade unions are being placed in a position of privilege that had previously been surpassed only by the monasteries in the Middle Ages.'

Howe was wounded at the demolition of his work in government. Not only was the Act being repealed but it was also blamed for being divisive and 'anti-union'. He had seen his legislation as merely equitable law.

The Wilson Government went back to the electorate in October 1974 with the Tories still in dutiful ranks supporting Mr Heath. The theme of the manifesto concentrated on the idea of a government of national unity, an idea first nourished by Jeremy Thorpe, the Liberal leader. The Tory manifesto coyly emphasized that although an incomes policy was essential, it was better if it were voluntary, an odd blend of the crucial and the optional. The electorate was not convinced that it had much meaning.

As shadow Environment Minister, Margaret Thatcher was one of the few politicians to make a mark in a dull campaign with her price-controlling promise to peg mortgage interest rates at nine and a half per cent against the prevailing eleven per cent. Labour's denunciation of this market-rigging idea focused attention on her.

Labour got back with an overall majority of three, but with forty more MPs than the Tories. After two defeats in one year and three defeats in the ten years of his leadership, it seemed natural that Ted Heath's tenure would be challenged and backbench sentiment soon indicated that the Tories expected the former Prime Minister to submit himself for re-election. Since the Conservatives had only formalized their leadership election procedures in 1965, it would be only the second such contest in the history of the world's oldest party. The winner had to have an overall majority. Otherwise, a second ballot would be held with an opportunity for new candidates also to throw down their gauntlet.

While Geoffrey had done little to distance himself from the policies adopted by the Tories since 1972, Sir Keith Joseph had begun to make a series of speeches marking out his own regret about what had happened and pointing out errors which should be avoided in future. In particular he highlighted the mistake of thinking that inflation was caused by shop stewards or businessmen or Arabs. He stated it was simply caused by the state spending more than it received in various forms of tax. In the meantime, together with Sir Keith, Margaret Thatcher had set up a new Tory think-tank called the Centre for Policy Studies. Although its resources were tiny, the venture began to create the necessary separation from the Heath leadership and the former Tory Government.

Howe offered his first public thoughts on the dual defeats of 1974 by saying self-examination should be conducted in terms of principles not personalities and observed that the art of politics was far more subtle than mere market research and salesmanship. He noted the defeat of the party had been reflected in a generalized loss of voter support amongst young and old, Scottish and Welsh, rural and urban. The Tory Party, he said, must not merely step to the left to outbid the Labour Party for votes. It ought not to compromise itself merely for office. The right ideas had to be applied.

In his first direct criticism of the Chancellor of the Exchequer in what was to become a long-running verbal boxing fight between Geoffrey Howe and Denis Healey, there was contemptuous reference to the Labour Minister's admission that he never saved a penny.

Few, if any, betting men in October 1974 would have imagined that Mrs Thatcher would bid to succeed Mr Heath. At the first ballot she led the former Prime Minister by 130 to 119, with Hugh Fraser on sixteen. Eleven Tories abstained. It was a secret ballot and Geoffrey Howe has not said how he voted. In the second ballot however he put his hat in the ring. He is not a man to plot and has never had a network of cronies or intimates. There was no ready band of Howe-ites. But he inspires respect and trust and has a large number of friends, many dating from the Bow Group. Fellow Wykehamist Ian Gow, David Walder, Elaine Kellett-Bowman and Antony Buck (Cambridge as well as Bow Group) served as an instant sales team for the Howe bid. No one had any illusions he might win. But the decision to stand for the first time marked him down as a politician aiming for the top.

'A number of parliamentary colleagues have urged me to put my name forward in the second ballot for the leadership of the Conservative Party,' he declared in a statement on 5

February, 1975. 'I am grateful for their support and advice. It is clear that the party must now unite under a new leader in presenting the country with the case for the free society. That society must be founded upon realistic economic policies. And it must be one that cares about every citizen.

'The case for that kind of Conservatism needs to be argued forthrightly – and with understanding, compassion and candour. Plainly I wish to play a leading part in that campaign. Whatever may be the shortcomings of the present electoral procedure, it is clearly intended, on the second ballot, to provide for a range of choice between possible alternatives. It can also serve to indicate the degree of support within the parliamentary party for different styles of leadership. With all these arguments in mind, I have agreed to let my name go forward as a candidate in the second ballot for the leadership of the Conservative Party.'

The real battle was fought between Mrs Thatcher and William Whitelaw. To Margaret Thatcher's 146 and Mr Whitelaw's 76 Howe shared third place, along with Jim Prior, at nineteen votes each. As a loyal colleague he had not sought Mr Heath's defeat. In terms of policy analysis Mrs Thatcher had far more modest credentials than Geoffrey Howe. His output of articles, speeches and papers since Bow Group days greatly exceeded hers. He could claim broader experience of ministerial office, if not actual Cabinet seniority, but since he had not challenged Mr Heath he could only be a token candidate. His reward came quickly. Instead of the expected invitation to Sir Keith Joseph as the natural economics spokesman, the new leader asked Geoffrey Howe to be shadow Chancellor. The decision came as a surprise but he was delighted to move away from roles with a high legal content and looked forward to the authority his status would give him in directing the public thinking of the Conservative Party. Both Peter Walker, his former political boss in the Department of Trade and Industry, and Geoffrey Rippon, colleague in the European negotiations, refused to serve in Mrs Thatcher's first shadow Cabinet.

While the world was intrigued by the selection of the first woman to lead a British political party; events at home moved on; and Howe became absorbed in the campaign relating to the Common Market referendum. As he travelled around the country to speaking engagements, he began to speak with relish. He denied that British sovereignty was threatened. He denied that Britain's flow of trade had been adversely affected by tariff barriers against the rest of the world. He denied that the Common Agricultural Policy was increasing food prices. He endorsed Denis Healey's view that problems in the United Kingdom economy stemmed from Europe. He said repeatedly, as he tried to whip up the pro-EEC vote, that the Common Market was about security and peace as much as trade. He was on the winning side. Britain voted soundly to stay inside the Community.

One of the factors attributing to Mrs Thatcher's victory within the parliamentary party was her scorching attack on capital transfer taxes. It fell to her new shadow Chancellor to begin his long duel with Chancellor Healey by delivering a sustained and detailed critique of the legislation. Howe's dogged and professorial harassing of Healey never mellowed into off-stage friendship. Howe thought of Healey as a rogue lacking in integrity of purpose, Healey dismissed Howe as a dullard and a bore. He christened Howe 'Mogadon Man' for the narcoleptic quality of some Commons performances. His cruel metaphor, that to be attacked by Geoffrey Howe was 'like being savaged by a dead sheep', caught public and political imagination and memory with its explicit, if unoriginal, imagery and was comparable to Foot's dismissal of Norman Tebbit as 'a semi-house-trained polecat'. No one now remembers the context in which Healey first referred to Howe as having ploughed through the tedious and tendentious farrago of moth-eaten cuttings presented to him by the Conservative Research Department. 'I must say,' he added, 'that part of his speech was rather like being savaged by a dead sheep.' Even he cannot have known how damaging the description would be at the time or that it would be resuscitated whenever the going got rough, such as the lengthy row over the Government Communications Headquarters in Cheltenham in 1984. It was the phrase of a taunting bully, who perhaps appreciated the intellectual power of the man he faced across the chamber and wished to score points, or if possible achieve a knockout while he could. By all accounts Healey did well, for the capsule description helped to conceal Howe's real qualities from many commentators, who found his presentation dull, took the phrase at face value and looked no further. The Howes were nevertheless cheered by one Canadian correspondent who wrote to them saying that to be savaged by dead sheep was no fun. She had been – when a joint of lamb fell onto her foot out of the freezer.

Geoffrey Howe's talents are not best used in Opposition. He lacks the punchy oratory which hits headlines. On the other hand, he enjoys the facilities which come with political power in Whitehall as well as the chance of achievement and change. He has admitted that the loss of the resources of a private office and use of a government car slowed his formidable productivity.

The Howes have never been wealthy. Sir Geoffrey probably could have been – had he stayed at the Bar instead of using it as a springboard to his political career. And this time he used the period of Opposition to return only part-time to the legal world where his services were in demand as a consultant. He is a lawyer's lawyer and as a former Solicitor-General as well as a QC, he ranked as one of the most eminent of silks. Now that he was shadow Chancellor, Howe needed more time for political planning. His frontline role had made an impression and he was invited to join the board of the Sun Alliance and London Insurance Company, a role which gave him greater insight into the Labour Government's plans for a new state pension scheme. AGB Research, a leading market research company, offered him a directorship after the October election and in 1976 EMI Ltd, the electronics and entertainment company, also invited him to join the board. Unlike some non-executive directors, particularly at a time when organizations still indulged in a fatter, more comfortable style of work, he took his duties seriously. Back in office however he is basically dependent on his salary as Foreign Secretary and, compared to many Tories of such rank, Geoffrey Howe's resources remain limited. One of the more assured toffs of the party was to say of the Howes' evident enjoyment of Chevening, the official residence in Kent: 'So nice to see the middle classes prospering.'

Geoffrey Howe has always been among the most prolific pamphleteers amongst politicians of any party, the majority of his papers being published by either the Bow Group or by the Conservative Political Centre, the Conservative Central Office agency which tries to nourish the uncharacteristic Tory habit of policy discussion. As a master policy proponent Howe was invited to be national president of the CPC in 1977. It is a minor irritation that he has yet to be offered the greatest CPC accolade, the lecture at the party conference.

The Howe family and his close colleagues remember the Opposition years as a hard slog, mastering and developing new economic policy. With the exception of the enterprise zone idea the shadow Chancellor kept a fairly low profile. In 1975 he opposed Mr Healey's sudden decision to raise VAT to 25 per cent on selected 'luxury' goods. He said: 'Such a new imposition would be the last straw for small businesses and would need 3,000 new customs officials to administer. Many people are so appalled by the prospect and it could provoke anger on such a scale that the entire tax-collecting machinery might be placed in peril.' Four years later Howe himself, by then Chancellor, was receiving equally fierce criticisms for increasing VAT to fifteen per cent. But this move had allowed substantial cuts in income tax and the principle of one flat rate had been advertized.

In the very beginning of the Labour Government public expenditure was allowed to accelerate but, after Mr Wilson retired, Jim Callaghan and then Healey tried to wrench the state's spending back and introduce more financially prudent principles. The International Monetary Fund developed an urgent interest in Britain's public book-keeping. It is scarcely surprising that Howe offered Healey no words of praise. He regarded him as a Socialist and dangerous and, latterly, as little more than a caricature of his former self playing for laughs and applause. The many years these two opposed each other, first over finance and the economy and then moving onto foreign affairs, produced little warmth or fellow feeling. But they are very different. Healey, brilliant but brash, bombastic and a verbal bully, put on the better initial show. But that now seems empty, his star having waned as Howe's has gained strength as courageous decisions in office have begun to have their effect.

The Opposition years provided an opportunity to leave

behind the policies and practice of the 1972 to 1974 period. Mrs Thatcher and Sir Keith Joseph welcomed the thought of a further attempt at bringing trade unions back within the rule of law and, although it was not his brief, Howe was active in sketching out the reforms that a successful Tory Party would apply. The Centre for Policy Studies remained a Thatcherite preserve and Howe, who had been very close during Bow Group years, turned again towards the Institute of Economic Affairs. Lord Harris of High Cross, its then director, recalls that he would send Geoffrey Howe all its publications and suggest additional reading for the future Chancellor. Ralph Harris regarded Howe as something of a lost soul who had been retrieved to the cause but he would often find that Howe had already devoured and absorbed the relevant texts of reviving liberal thinking. A proponent of the market economy, Harris regarded the Heath years as catastrophic, not just in policy terms but also in the history of policy ideas. Markets had seemed to be in permanent eclipse by 1974 with the Tories as dedicated to central control as the Labour Party.

The years of Opposition hardened Geoffrey Howe's resolve to be a reforming and simplifying Chancellor if chance came his way. He became a severe critic of the British tax system. 'Our tax regime is far too complex,' he said in one speech. 'Businessmen are bewildered by our fiscal labyrinth. No ordinary citizen can understand the confusion. This chaos is compounded by continuous change. Ten new taxes in ten years have reduced many taxpayers to gibbering resentment. CGT, CTT, SET, VAT, betterment levy, development land tax, two different forms of corporation tax and petroleum tax.'

His speeches and articles were delivered at a remarkable rate. Howe enjoys travelling and even looks forward to a sleeper journey – except perhaps, as happened when Chancellor, evening trousers and wallet vanish from the overnight train to much merriment and publicity. The trousers were recovered by the rail side, the wallet never. He is particularly attracted to student audiences since he feels they are more alert to new ideas than the normally obedient party workers and that one young man or woman converted to the cause of liberty makes the journey worthwhile. He also has a natural disposition to accept invitations to Wales. His engagement diary was wider than even Mrs Thatcher's and he kept this pace up until the 1979 election. If the Conservatives ever opened their electoral college for the leadership wider than the parliamentary party, Howe, after his years of conscientious addresses to party members, would have a huge advantage. His range is impressive. He could lecture learned societies on their specialization or come up with light, mocking speeches with simple words. One day it might be an international tax experts conference, the next he might be teasing an audience with childlike parables about corner shops, run by Maggie or Jim, and how they would prosper differently.

With a variety of themes, Geoffrey Howe stated that public spending was not matched by income; taxation was oppressive; enterprise neutered, and state industry vastly inefficient. He even touched on the possibilities of alternatives to local authority supplied schooling and different ways of funding health. But his language was so circumspect and reserved that neither the party nor Fleet Street ever really heard or understood the bold ideas which were later to emerge as generic Thatcherism. His junior Treasury spokesman, David Howell, coined the word 'privatisation' in tandem with Sir Geoffrey. Until then commitments had been to denationalization and they were so compromised that only one undertaking appeared in the 1979 manifesto. Uninspiring to the non-cognoscenti it may be, but the National Freight Corporation has of course proved one of the great successes of management buyouts and employee share ownership. Howell says of Geoffrey Howe that his courage and the clarity of his ideas are never appreciated except by his closest friends. Leon Brittan, a close colleague and also a Bow Group apostle, says that the quiet and self-effacing manner is not a political failing. It is simply the way the man is made.

Throughout his period as shadow Treasury spokesman he was constantly overshadowed by Mrs Thatcher. Although some of his friends felt she sometimes lacked the proper courtesies of consultation, Margaret Thatcher, as well as benefiting from her status as Britain's first female parliamentary leader, was the more vivid presence. She was also a prospective prime minister and her words naturally attracted constant interest. She also had a team of speech writers while Geoffrey Howe, although welcoming ideas and even drafts, always wrote his own texts.

As the Labour Government struggled to rein in its finances and placate the IMF, Howe's speeches grew ever more contemptuous. For many years he had feared and disliked Socialism. As well as the intellectual error he had believed it to be since the 1940s, he now saw it increasingly as a threat to security and values. Each taunt by Healey and each dismissal by Callaghan hardened Howe in his intention to be a strong Chancellor. He relished describing ministers as no more than footmen for the union bosses. Any temporary concordat between unions and government he dismissed as laughable. The Callaghan Government was to be humiliated as the Heath Government had been. With or without an incomes policy the trade unions were still able to despoil the economy.

By the new year of 1979, the lorry drivers were on strike, workers in the National Health Service were going on intermittent strikes and pickets were preventing supplies reaching hospitals. In addition, rubbish piled up in the streets to cause widespread revulsion. Mr Callaghan seemed as incapable of dealing with the chaos as Mr Heath had been. But for Mr Callaghan and for Mr Foot it was even more cruel of providence to be humbled in this way.

Nevertheless, it was not the so-called 'winter of discontent' which actually broke the fragile Callaghan Government. The Welsh and Scottish Nationalists, who had fourteen votes in the House of Commons, had induced the Government to offer Home Rule to Wales and Scotland, subject only to local referenda. In neither case was Home Rule carried and the Government lost the subsequent vote of confidence on 23 March. The election in May gave the Tories a majority of forty-three, with a lead over Labour of two million votes. Geoffrey and Elspeth Howe left Fentiman Road south of the river for No 11 Downing Street.

It had been a period for the regeneration of ideas, of application and patience. One notion did however capture Geoffrey Howe's imagination as encapsulating something of his vision for the future of the country. Enterprise was not then so fashion-

127

able in word or deed and the idea of an enterprise zone positively quixotic. But he was convinced that with some such venture, as well as tax cuts, could lie the seeds of real incentive, changing attitudes and positive action.

13

Enterprise

Three thousand red, white and blue balloons soared into the air above London's docklands as Sir Geoffrey Howe, Chancellor of the Exchequer, launched the new enterprise zone in the Isle of Dogs. A striped marquee had been erected beside the development corporation offices and buffet lunch provided to make sure the guests would enjoy their venture into the unknown lands of east London – and talk business. Otherwise the scene was totally derelict, a flattened moonscape studded with occasional derelict buildings and, in the background, council tower blocks. It was May 1982 in one of the most prosperous cities in the world.

Only four years earlier Sir Geoffrey, then shadow Chancellor, had visited the same Isle of Dogs one summer evening to speak at a special Bow Group dinner. After twenty-five years, the group, by then part of the younger Tory political establishment, had decided to return to the area in which it held its first meetings and asked its most famous member, former chairman and editor of *Crossbow* to be principal guest at a dinner in the Waterman's Arms, Glengarnock Road. He used the occasion to launch an idea which has since crossed the Atlantic and which in Britain could be claimed as the political spring of the country's recent enterprise culture. It was an idea which Sir Geoffrey had been nourishing and developing for some time. He had then unexpectedly found someone else working along similar lines. This was geography professor Peter Hall, then a Labour supporter and intellectual maverick of the planning world. Long before such opinions bubbled to the surface, let alone became fashionable, Hall had dared to suggest that Britain might not have been the sick man of Europe if industry had been allowed to expand in the south. Instead, growth there was barred by planning regulations and the Government tried to steer development with grants into other regions, regardless of their suitability.

In the summer of 1978 the Isle of Dogs in the loop of the Thames was not recognizably in the same nation as the bustling City of London only two and a half miles to the west. The docks had closed after years of strife, leaving hundreds of acres of dereliction and decay. Desolation had multiplied as warehouses were left empty, cafés shut, pubs lost the majority of their customers and local people lost their traditional livelihood. In the borough of Tower Hamlets, then one of the most entrenched Labour areas in the country, eighty-eight per cent of families lived in council houses and flats, seventy-eight per cent on some form of welfare dependency.

It was in these surroundings that Sir Geoffrey launched his revolutionary thesis. Indeed, Conservative Central Office was sufficiently concerned and careful to offer a two-page note explaining that the speech was purely Sir Geoffrey's own idea and nothing to do with official Opposition party policy. But it was an outstanding contribution and thrilling, even cheeky, in its backing for the totally new notion of enterprise zones. The idea challenged the normal assumptions about the role of government and its agencies in planning and directing development; assumptions which had dominated the intellectual scene for the previous forty years. It attacked red tape with a vengeance, the principle that Whitehall or the Town Hall knows best. It dared to suggest that the country might do better if it set the people free. It proposed development corporations in inner-city areas; not for public development, as had been the practice with Britain's new towns, but to assemble land for sale to the private sector. In the third Thatcher Government, with so much change in outlook and attitudes, it is difficult to appreciate how extraordinarily novel, if not bizarre, the Isle of Dogs speech was at the time. None of his senior colleagues publicly associated themselves with it and many scoffed at its exuberance. Few politicians come up with new ideas of their own. This one blazed a trail and, even more unusually, the man with the original concept was the man who transformed the policy into practice.

Of course, the speech had the characteristic qualities of its author. It was reasonable and polite. It contained references to the wide circle of personal contacts he enjoys from squatters to planners and included the usual quota of mock colloquialisms and Latin tags. But it served as a manifesto for Geoffrey Howe's vision of a liberal state and as a foretaste of what he would attempt as Chancellor of the Exchequer following the subsequent Tory election victory in 1979.

'Almost ten years ago, I was walking with a Labour councillor, whom I know well, down a road in Poplar,' he began. 'As we passed by a terrace of decaying houses two up and two down and about a hundred years old, he observed: "Are those not a dreadful monument to private landlordism?" "Absolutely not," I replied. "The fact that they are here in such numbers is a tribute to the speed with which nineteenth century private enterprise housed the newly urbanised working people to standards much higher than they had previously enjoyed. The fact they are now decaying is a testimony to rent control, municipalisation and other manifestations of political folly." My councillor friend was not convinced. But I think I did open a window in his mind.'

Since then, Howe went on, the site had been cleared but remained vacant, part of the urban wilderness, dereliction and devastation, which equally affected Merseyside, the Clyde, Manchester, Leeds and the West Midlands. Even where rebuilding had taken place, many businesses and most of the jobs had gone, along with far too many of the younger and more energetic inhabitants.

He continued: 'All this is part of Britain's wider problem. For some years now our economy has been sliding into decline. Our living standards have been falling relative to the rest of the world. Seediness is the order of the day. While whole communities have been blitzed by "planning" and stagnation, whole industries have fallen off the edge of our economic table and the business and industries of the future have not sprung

131

up in their place. Look out of the train window on a journey in any corner of Britain and you can see the dangerous extent to which we have been living off the industrial and social capital that was accumulated by earlier generations and failing to amass our own.'

This was the key to understanding the developing sickness of society, he went on. The consequent lack of economic success was breeding social tensions and threatening to destroy the framework of civilized existence. In the face of such problems two distinct political philosophies were on offer. The Socialists offered state direction of resources, trade unions in partnership with a less than entrepreneurial political élite and capital for development funded through taxation. This, he said, would lead eventually to an increasingly sullen and seedy economy with authoritarianism as an inevitable consequence. The second alternative was the libertarian approach. It did not involve the outright rejection of a role for public authorities but looked to private initiative, widely dispersed and properly rewarded, for the mainspring of the economy. In many areas the burgeoning of state activity positively frustrated many healthy initiatives. Over-regulation was a major part of Britain's private disease. Countries with the fastest-rising living standards, like Taiwan, South Korea, Hong Kong and Singapore, operated their economies in a manner which was the nearest to this ideal.

'Of course the State can point to some apparent successes,' Sir Geoffrey said. 'Britain's post-war new towns have promoted the growth of prosperous communities. But it is anything but clear that their capital costs have even been counted properly ... In other more complex areas, the more the State has become involved the less obvious its success in hitting even those targets for which the original plan was designed. For a quarter of a century the centre of my home town in South Wales saw its commercial life ebbing away while "plan" succeeded "plan" ... Even the prosperity of county communities is now being stifled by structure plans which set out ruthlessly to limit future commercial activity to businesses that are already based within the county. Is it not perverse to be tearing down tariff barriers within Europe at the same time as we are erecting ring fences to prevent the movement of enterprises within our own country

'But it is in the big cities,' he continued, 'that the appetite of the State has almost outrun its capacity. In Liverpool in December 1976, 1,100 acres of inner city land (one-third of the total) lay vacant. But only 150 of these were included in any firm programme for development. A third of all this vacant land was allocated to highways, none of which were likely to be implemented. Half of this land had been vacant for five years.' The same situation existed in many other major cities, Sir Geoffrey said and added: 'The public purse has been quite unable to provide the funds or the enterprise to match the planners' aspirations ... This is the background against which successive governments have introduced Bill after Bill and shuffled much the same amount of money from one new fashionably named urban programme to another. But all attempts to reform seem only to multiply the bureaucracy ... The local MP, Ian Mikardo, apostle of an entirely planned Socialist society, has rightly defined the effect of planning on his constituency (in Tower Hamlets): "One does nothing until one is absolutely sure that it is right. Since it takes many years to ensure that one is doing the right thing one does not do anything at all for many years." Tacitus put it more crisply – he was describing the Roman scorched earth policy in first century Germany: "Faciunt solitudinem, pacem appellant." (They make a desert, they call it peace.)

'But of course London docklands is only one example. The frustrating domination of more and more of our urban communities by a combination of widespread public land ownership and public intervention into virtually all private activities has produced a form of municipal mortmain which will not be shifted without a huge effort of will.'

Howe went on to say that before Henry VIII dissolved the monasteries, it had proved necessary to pass the statutes of mortmain specifically to prevent land being held idle in moribund monastic ownership. 'Today's prelates, at once the leaders and the prisoners of municipal monasticism, are in town and county halls or the head offices of nationalised industries and public corporations. I do not question their goodwill and sense of commitment to "the public interest". Just as zealously as the monks and abbots strove to do the will of God, today's chief executives and planning officers seek to serve

133

the will of democracy – but alas with fruitless results. In the outcome tens of thousands of people are unwillingly involved in frustrating each other's efforts, as well as those of their fellow citizens. I sadly echo the comment of one frustrated planner that "One is forced to question the current priorities of a system of planning which spends so much time and energy exercising strict controls over the extensions of individual houses and minor changes of use, while allowing whole areas to be demolished and laid to waste for years, even decades, at the heart of the most populous cities in the country."

It was time, Howe said, for a change of approach, to restore competitive diversity, to reward inventiveness, marketing and development. The return to economic vitality crucially depended upon fundamental tax reform, including tax cuts to allow the rapid accumulation of post-tax wealth by that comparatively small band of people who had the capacity to identify and exploit new commercial opportunities.

'That is why we must restore the legitimacy of becoming rich by taking risks – apart from those which arise from doing the football pools,' Sir Geoffrey said. That was the way to promote the creation of real jobs. But sensible deregulation was almost as urgent – not of consumer protection or against racial discrimination but economic interventionism, such as price and dividend control, the consequences of the planning system and the paraphernalia of industrial and office development permits. But, he went on: 'One must be very doubtful whether these general changes will bring speedy or sufficient relief to the worst afflicted areas. Some might even argue that they are beyond help and would abandon them as inner city ghost towns – a doleful monument to our collective incompetence. That would be a feckless and inhuman conclusion.'

If these areas were the biggest challenge, he wondered whether they could become the greatest opportunities. Public enterprise, he said, had certainly not delivered the goods. The original prosperity of cities had been founded on the pursuit of profit. Should we not again seek a solution based primarily on the view that those who helped restore prosperity were entitled to expect financial reward on a substantial scale. 'Unless people are able to earn and keep significant reward for the investment and effort that we wish them to put into

Geoffrey Howe was knighted on becoming Solicitor General in the Heath Government. Seen here with Lady Howe, their elder daughter Caroline and the twins, Alec and Amanda, when he was sworn in in June 1970.

The new Chancellor of the Exchequer leaves 11 Downing Street to present his first budget in 1979.

(*Above*) The men most closely involved in the 1982 budget. From right to left round the table, first the political team of the Treasury with Jock Bruce-Gardyne, economic secretary, Nicholas Ridley, financial secretary, Geoffrey Howe, Chancellor of the Exchequer, Leon Brittan, chief secretary, John Wakeham and Barney Hayhoe, both ministers of state. Continuing on round come John Kerr, then Sir Geoffrey's private secretary and now head of the European section in the Foreign Office, Sir Geoffrey Littler, permanent secretary in charge of international finance, Sir Terence Burns, chief economic adviser, Sir Douglas Wass, senior permanent secretary, and Sir Anthony Rawlinson, permanent secretary in charge of public spending.

(*Above opposite*) Howe is a favourite at Tory Party conferences and receives long standing ovations, as in 1982 when he was Chancellor of the Exchequer. Others on the platform include Margaret Thatcher, Leon Brittan, Norman Tebbit (second row) and Lord Cockfield on his right and Cecil Parkinson and Elspeth Howe (second row) to his left.

(*Opposite left*) In May 1982 as Chancellor, Geoffrey Howe returned to the Isle of Dogs, where he had first proposed the enterprise zone idea at a Bow Group meeting, to launch the London zone. Sir Nigel Broackes, chairman of the London Docklands Development Corporation, is standing immediately to the right.

(*Opposite right*) A Christmas party for handicapped children at No. 11 Downing Street at which the Chancellor of the Exchequer really could play the role of Santa Claus.

Sir Geoffrey and Lady Howe talking to former prime minister Harold Macmillan, the Earl of Stockton, at a dinner of the United and Cecil Club.

The Foreign Secretary, alongside Deng Xiaoping, applauds the signing of the Hong Kong agreement by Mrs Thatcher and the then prime minister, Zhao Ziyang, in the Great Hall of the People in Beijing on 19 December 1984.

A meeting between the British Foreign Secretary and Ronald Reagan,
President of the United States, in July 1983.

Formal international meetings feature regularly ... Geoffrey Howe and
George Shultz, United States Secretary of State.

Mikhail Gorbachev being welcomed by Geoffrey Howe for talks at Hampton Court on his first visit to Britain in December 1984, before he became leader of the Soviet Union.

Treaty signing in Moscow in March 1987 ... the Foreign Secretary and Eduard Shevardnadze, his Russian opposite number, were watched by their two leaders, Mrs Thatcher and Mikhail Gorbachev (to the left behind Sir Geoffrey).

Carnival time on a visit to Bonn, Western Germany, with Minister for Foreign Affairs, Hans-Dietrich Genscher.

'The Rt. Hon'ble Sir Geoferely' in Chohatna Bichpuri, Agra and the foundation stone he unveiled on 1 April 1986.

FOUNDATION STONE
OF
COMMUNITY CENTRE LAID IN
VILLAGE CHOHATNA BICHPURI AGRA
BY
Rt. HON'BLE SIR GEOFERELY
BRITISH SECRETARY OF STATE FOR
FOREIGN AND COMMON WEALTH AFFAIRS.
1 st APRIL 1986

The Foreign Secretary walking with Lord Bruce-Gardyne at Chevening.

Geoffrey and Elspeth Howe with their grandson Christopher and Budget, their second Jack Russell terrier.

our urban deserts, they are just not going to be interested,' he said. 'More pleasant, they may well feel, to run an antique shop in Winchester or a restaurant at Aldeburgh.

'Against this background,' he went on, 'I was delighted last year to discover that a distinguished Socialist, Professor Peter Hall, was beginning to reach for the same prescription as myself – and I emphasize that I am now offering a purely personal view. Why not, he argued – and so do I – consider unorthodox methods? Why not aim to create the Hong Kong of the 1950s inside inner Liverpool or inner Glasgow? Small selected areas of inner cities, he argued, should be simply thrown open to all kinds of initiatives with minimal control – based on the idea of "fairly shameless free enterprise". The germ of this revolutionary idea springs from the experience of other communities where something like a freeport solution has laid the foundations of economic liberation. Independent countries like Hong Kong and Singapore have been entirely free to make themselves magnets for enterprise, with generally benevolent tax and customs regimes, freedom from exchange control and an absence of unnecessary regulations and of heavy social or other obligations on commerce and industry. Special tax and other concessions for pioneer businesses have been guaranteed for a substantial period of time.' On a more modest scale, West Berlin, Shannon and even the Channel Islands and the Isle of Man offered a similar approach, Sir Geoffrey said.

There were three concepts: the freeport or free trade zone; Professor Hall's 'Crown Colony', a largely independent community free from tariffs and exempt from most legislation including the welfare state; and his own suggestion for the enterprise zone, which he believed to be well worth studying.

The whole idea, Sir Geoffrey said, would be to designate in four or five places, such as Clydeside, Merseyside, the West Midlands and east London, substantial areas of land for development with as much freedom as possible to make profits and create jobs. Moving onto the key elements, he said: 'Planning control of any detailed kind would cease to apply. Any building that complied with very basic anti-pollution, health and safety standards and that was not over a stated maximum height – that "did not threaten to frighten the horses in the

135

streets" – would be permissible for any lawful purpose. IDCs and ODPs (industrial and office development permits) would not be required.

'Second, the Community Land Act would be put effectively into reverse. Public authorities which owned land would be required within a specified time to dispose of it to private bidders by auction in the open market. New developments in the area would be free from rent control. Third, entrepreneurs who moved into this land would be granted exemption from development land tax and perhaps exemption from rates in whole or in part.

'Fourth, business in the areas in question should be given a guarantee that tax law – affecting investment, depreciation and so on – would not be changed to their disadvantage. And they should be entitled to an undertaking from the Crown that they would not be liable to any future proposal for nationalization. No government grants or subsidies would be payable to any enterprise within the area. Fifth, certain other legal obligations or threats should be declared not to operate within the area: price control and pay policy, for example. There are other pieces of legislation that could be stated not to apply – such as some or all of the provisions of the Employment Protection Act. Sixth, all conditions would be guaranteed for a stated and substantial number of years.'

Sir Geoffrey went on to suggest a new management authority something like a new town corporation. 'My kind of agency,' he said, 'would not be acquiring property for the public sector but disposing of it for private development. Existing inhabitants might be given a share of the action: a right to an equity stake in the new authority ... I hope we shall find communities queuing up to apply for enterprise zone status. Meanwhile my proposals are not intended to be a politically exclusive idea but an experiment that could fire the imagination of people in all parties or in none. I believe it would be worthwhile ensuring that part of any enterprise zone could be available to non-commercial groups who wished to establish workers' co-operatives – Mondrago fashion or any other. If the Tribune Group or the Socialist Workers' Party wanted part of an enterprise zone to themselves – well, why not?"

The Isle of Dogs enterprise zone speech predicted so much

that was to follow. Although the language is soft-spoke, he outlined a revolutionary approach to the economy in general, and in particular the regeneration of the inner city – with special agencies undercutting the dead hand of bureaucracy, forced sale of publicly-owned land, reduced planning control and financial incentives. It included a hint of the abolition of exchange control, which allowed Britons to buy and hold foreign assets without central bank permission; which some think his greatest achievement as Chancellor and which most people now take for granted. It also contained the seeds of the dissolution of the metropolitan counties and the Greater London Council and the enforced contracting out of many functions got its first airing. But only one national newspaper was really excited. *The Sunday Express* predicted Hong Kongs in every port city. Political columnists and broadcasters generally failed to spot the Bow Group paper as a menu for the future. Other members of the Tory Party kept quiet; some thought it impractical.

Yet two years later, in his second budget, Sir Geoffrey announced his plans to set up, on an experimental basis, about half a dozen enterprise zones. It had taken him a long time to sell the idea to Margaret Thatcher but he managed to persuade her that this could be an effective alternative to existing regional policy. Then there were tortuous inter-departmental discussions in Whitehall as the civil servants dissected the proposals. As tends to happen, there were changes, as indeed there have been in their operation. The forced sale of vacant land for example became a separate measure to apply to all local authorities. The ability to opt out of rent control vanished. No means was provided for local people to share in the equity. But the creation of a special planning regime survived and developers can opt out of the planning process if they conform to local parameters individually drawn up for each zone. Originally, before its abolition, no development land tax was payable and occupants enjoy relief from local rates for the ten-year life of all zones. Firms were also freed from obligations to produce certain statistics for government. The main innovation was the decision to give capital tax allowances on all new building and refurbishment for business, which basically means that profitable companies can offset virtually the whole cost of construction against any liability for corporation tax.

Cities queued up for the privilege and a total of twenty-five enterprise zones were declared in scenes of apparent hopelessness following major industrial closure, such as docks and steel works. They are located in all parts of the United Kingdom – Swansea, Milford Haven, Clydebank, Invergordon, Tayside, Tyneside, north-west Kent, including the former naval docks at Chatham, and, of course, the Isle of Dogs.

The relaxation of planning has in some areas led to the creation of new, American-style shopping centres with vast areas of parking; a style of development long resisted by the planning fraternity in their concern for existing city centres and people who do not have the use of a car. Tyneside now boasts Europe's largest out-of-town shopping centre, complete with themed leisure complex for people who want to extend their day out with funfair rides, miniature golf and puppets. And the centre of Newcastle-upon-Tyne still flourishes. Merry Hill, Dudley, is set to provide similar facilities. Zones saw the launching of the business unit, a building which could be used as an office or for small-scale production, whereas planning until recently still insisted on precise definition and, only with the consent of bureaucracy, the possibility of change of use. By the end of 1986 there were 5,600 people employed in Corby's zone where there had been but sixty-one. In the twenty-three British zones about 33,000 more men and women had jobs and there were some 1,450 additional workplaces or firms. About sixty per cent of new jobs in British enterprise zones have been in manufacturing.

On the Isle of Dogs, a new light railway, with two-car trains in bright blue and orange livery, now snakes its way above the three West India Docks and gently curves alongside yet more water. Modern streamlined buildings stand in the immediate vicinity, trimmed in primary colours. One houses the *Daily Telegraph*, another the *Guardian*'s printing works, another a firm of accountants, another a publishing firm. Tower cranes dominate surrounding building sites. Millions of square feet of offices are promised including the controversial twelve million square scheme with three towers proposed for Canary Wharf. Geoffrey Howe suggested a height limit which would not frighten the horses. In the Isle of Dogs the local planning regime set one of 100 feet but the Corporation then decided to throw such discretion to the winds and, in the excitement of success, even started selling off air rights over water in the docks they had said they would preserve. The wish or willingness to let developers build bigger and higher and at greater density without regard for the Exchequer, which means the taxpayer, has led to the rejection of further enterprise zones. They have quite simply become too expensive as government has totted up the bill for land, infrastructure, rates (which it pays to the town halls) and the 100 per cent tax shelter on virtually all building costs. After four years the figure had reached nearly £300 million with the development pipeline bulging with planned but unfinished projects. Sir Geoffrey Howe's idea, conceived at a time of economic decline, born at the point of change, and growing up in a much more adventurous, profitable climate had not only succeeded, it had succeeded too well.

14

The Chancellor Prescribes

The errors of the Heath Government inoculated many of his former ministers against any predeliction for past policies. Margaret Thatcher, Geoffrey Howe and Keith Joseph, five years on, could see more clearly the causes of inflation and the corrosive anti-democratic influence of the trade unions. Incomes policies had been at the heart of political control for a generation and the new Chancellor now accepted this traditional approach would always lead to some form of union sell-out and effectively transfer power elsewhere than government. The proposed change of policy might mean higher unemployment in the short term but this could be presented as an inevitable result of sound monetarism, the failure of industrial modernization or international trends. Although no one put it so crudely, increased unemployment would help bring the unions under control.

'It is difficult now to remember conditions,' says Brendon Sewill, former director of the Conservative Research Department and a member of former Tory Chancellor Tony Barber's private office. 'But there seemed a very real possibility in the mid-1970s that Britain could become ungovernable, with inflation leading to ever-increasing wage demands, strikes and a collapse of the democratic system. Ultimately uncontrolled inflation might have led to some form of military or totalitarian government as happened in so many other countries in the world.' The risk was real and the alternative harsh. But stable prices were absolutely essential even if the necessary measures led to wide-scale unemployment. The Government was taking a chance and, in electoral terms, no one could know if sufficient benefits would come through in time to help the Tories to continue in power for another four or five years and continue their efforts to transform public attitudes and actions.

As they took over on the 4 May 1979, the Conservatives had a majority of forty-three seats and a swing in their favour of 5.2 per cent. It was Butskellism that they were replacing more than James Callaghan and his tired team. Most critics, not just the cynics, anticipated that prices and incomes policy and the whole merry-go-round of stop–go would return in due course whatever the rhetorical courtesies. As Chancellor, Sir Geoffrey Howe was expected to talk of free enterprise, lower taxes, sound money and a smaller role for the state, but there was a general assumption that Britain would stumble back to control on dividends, rents, profits and incomes and general state intervention.

Denis Healey's expansionary budget of 1978 was propelling inflation. Wages were rising and the incoming government had promised to award the public sector its generous index-linked wage claims. Although the promise of lower tax rates had been part of the Conservatives electoral appeal, Keynesian convention dictated that taxes would have to be increased and more money borrowed or printed. The Government also arrived in power with the nationalized industries, 'the fossilised sector of the economy', as Geoffrey Howe called them, dependent on large subsidies. Management was not expected to run such state corporations on profit-seeking lines, nor had the necessary powers.

The new Chancellor of the Exchequer presented his first budget only five weeks after arriving at the Treasury. The economic background was entirely gloomy. The May money supply figures showed that the volume of new money or credit entering the economy had risen by fourteen per cent, well above even Mr Healey's target range of eight to twelve per cent. The rate of inflation had reached double figures.

It was a memorable budget. Howe implemented practically all the recommendations of the Opposition tax committee and carried through a number of measures which would have been politically difficult, if not impossible, at a later stage in the life of the Government. Not only did he cut the standard rate of income tax from 33p to 30p in the pound and remove 1,300,000 people from the tax net by raising the thresholds, but he also slashed top rates from 83p to 60p, increased VAT from the two existing rates of eight and twelve and a half per cent to fifteen per cent and abolished exchange control. The cut in the highest personal tax rates was bigger than many people expected and than some people advised. Howe wanted to make a statement about rewards for enterprise in the new Britain. But to smooth the dramatic nature of the change, he cleverly apologized for not being able to do more for men and women in these categories, who were after all already the richer members of society.

State pensions were increased in accordance with election promises. In his speech he conceded: 'I cannot do as much as I should have liked and I cannot do as much as is needed ... Our long-term aim must be to reduce income tax to a basic rate of no more than 25 pence.' However, the foundations had first to be laid through the control of inflation combined with incentives for new endeavour. Cumulatively, income tax cuts amounted to nearly £4,550 million but this was balanced by the jolt of the VAT increase and an extra 10p per gallon on petrol. The VAT rise alone pushed up the retail prices index by three per cent and just about paid for the income tax cuts. People kept more of what they earned but they paid more for goods. In addition, the very high rates of tax on investment income were reduced, prescription charges increased, dividend controls scrapped and public spending squeezed. The public sector borrowing requirement fell from £9.2 to £8.2 billion and the target for new money creation set between seven and eleven per cent. By 1987 that original £9.2 billion would have been about £38 billion. In fact it was down to £4 billion. Geoffrey Howe's first budget set the tone for the Thatcher years. John Biffen sums up his colleagues' views: 'I do not deny for one moment that Geoffrey's was a very severe package. The severity was made necessary by the situation we inherited.'

Prime ministers have always taken a direct and natural interest in economic policy. But in Margaret Thatcher, Geoffrey Howe had a leader who took a passionate, intimate and direct interest in Treasury affairs. 'For anyone else it would have been a strain and an intrusion, but Geoffrey had the patience to be unperturbed,' says an associate. The numerical dominance of the 'wets' – Prior, Pym, Gilmour, Carrington, Walker and St John Stevas, and monetary agnostics such as Hailsham or Carlisle – had the curious effect of transferring real decision-making about the economy away from the formal Cabinet to the 'E' committee. Meeting on Tuesday mornings, Mr Prior was the only non-monetarist to join the discussions. Cajoled by Mrs Thatcher, but subtly led by Howe, the 'E' committee was the centre of British government from May 1979. A further Cabinet committee, 'Misc 62', chaired by William Whitelaw, fielded the demands of the spending ministries.

British prime ministers are technically First Lords of the Treasury and the connecting door between No 10 and No 11 Downing Street can serve a very real purpose in achieving two-way communication of ideas and purpose. Margaret Thatcher would phone Geoffrey – or the other way round – and he could be with her almost instantly. In addition, Ian Gow, a fellow Wykehamist, Howe's leadership campaign manager and by then the Prime Minister's private parliamentary secretary, formed a friendly go-between.

A Cabinet colleague says of this time: 'We really met for ceremonial purposes. All power, all decision-taking, all policy formation occurred between No 10 and No 11. It seemed to mostly occur late at night as decisions unmade in the evening were often concluded by the morning. Mrs Thatcher and Howe could not have been closer. It wasn't a conspiracy because Keith Joseph would always endorse them and I don't think John Nott (then Trade Secretary) would ever dissent either. But Cabinet was not invited to decide. We were merely told what had been decided.'

During the early years of his Chancellorship, Geoffrey Howe was inhabiting a Treasury in which most senior mandarins were – or had been – Keynesian supporters, who had set out with the conviction that ideas of monetary continence were futile or harmful and that the art of good economic husbandry was only to modulate demand. The Prime Minister always made her impatience with the Treasury knights well known, but Geoffrey Howe was, as ever, studiously polite and he conscientiously read their papers on the macro-economic errors of the Government. It was a pointed repudiation of the Treasury's past that Howe brought in Professor Terry Burns of the London Business School to be Chief Economic Adviser. His expertise lay in international monetary studies and forecasting. He was a complete outsider. The Prime Minister and Chancellor also took advice from Professor Alan Walters and John Hoskyns, head of the No 10 policy unit. They worked in isolation but were clear-headed in their opposition to the sceptical, world-weary posture of the Treasury civil servants.

The £4 billion spending cuts Howe sought preoccupied most of his time for the next six months. The spending departments simply did not believe that the Chancellor would persist in seeking this scale of reduction from the public sector. From early on Geoffrey Howe held a meeting every morning with his junior ministers and special advisers with no civil servants present. The sense of cohesion and purpose they had as the central focus of government policy was strong, and esprit de corps was high, however adverse media criticism or unhappy the spending ministers.

Geoffrey Howe's role in the Tories' previous effort at trade union reform meant that he accompanied Employment Secretary, Jim Prior, to meetings with the Trades Union Congress in the summer of 1979. They were frosty but somewhat strange occasions because union leaders' distrust, if not fear, was concentrated, not on the departmental minister, but on the Chancellor. The TUC reckoned that Geoffrey Howe was as strong an influence on Prior as Mrs Thatcher. He shared her determination, although such views did not have public expression, that the unions must be tamed. They had defeated the original attempt to bring them within the law. This must not be allowed to happen again. When the Government issued a consultation paper on the reform of trade union law, the reaction was pretty predictable: 'Maximum resistance' promised by the Transport and General Workers and 'total opposition' from the TUC.

At that time Geoffrey Howe criticized unions who imagined 'a better future without having to do anything different or difficult about it; a dream world where we can have more public spending without higher taxes, higher interest rates or greater inflation; a dream world in which all this can be delivered by an economy whose manufacturing output is below its level of six years ago. It is a dream world in which there is no such thing as cause and effect ... in which people can be paid more without producing more; where earnings always go up in good times but never down in bad; where profits can be reduced but investment and living standards increased. Trade unions are not God-given. They are given by society, by the law, by the elected government. If they are used to do economic damage and inflict human suffering, it is legitimate to question their scope.'

The Tories permitted free collective bargaining, which the unions had asked from the Callaghan Government. But the Treasury, under Howe's guidance, would not authorize any extra public expenditure to pay for wage increases. Pay rises to civil servants and teachers, as promised by the Clegg Commission, combined with higher prices arising from the new level of VAT, led to renewed demands. It appeared at first that monetarism made absolutely no difference. Then, when the Government stood firm and provided no extra cash to finance the increases, the public services had to cut back on staff. The unions had priced their members out of jobs. In his mild-mannered way Geoffrey Howe was entirely ruthless. If there was any political omission, it lay in not persuading parliamentary colleagues of the high seriousness of what he and Mrs Thatcher were determined to do. Only by 1980 did commentators come to appreciate that the previous commitment to full employment of virtually all post-war governments had quietly been abandoned. There had been some recognition that full employment was a major factor in inflation under Callaghan and unemployment increased from about one million to 1,500,000; but nothing like the numbers which were already in train.

In his March 1980 budget, Sir Geoffrey launched the medium-term financial strategy, the nearest the Government came to a formal explanation of monetarism – so that people would know it would last over a number of years and adjust their behaviour accordingly. Devoted to controlling inflation that budget saw public spending cut by a further £1,000 million and some tax thresholds were raised. Howe's enterprise zone brainchild was incorporated, but had little popular appeal. Generally, the budget was poorly received in the Conservative Party and criticized by academics who emphasized the rising rate of inflation, by then touching twenty per cent. It reached twenty-two per cent in May. Although money supply had fallen, the situation did not match up with the official deflationary posture. Corporatist critics of Howe policies included both the Confederation of British Industry and the TUC. But from June 1980 the rate of inflation began to fall reaching a level of three and a half per cent in early 1988 with only a few blips along the way. But that situation still lay in the future.

Although at the 1980 party conference it was generally expected that the Government would indicate a willingness for some compromise, Mrs Thatcher said: 'You turn if you want to. The lady's not for turning.' Geoffrey Howe's speech was not popular. He was unable to offer any promise of further tax cuts nor any compromise on his public spending strategy and his autumn statement in November that year foreshadowed increased taxation and continued cuts in public expenditure. He argued: 'I am determined that the PSBR (borrowing requirement) in 1981–2 should be consistent with the Government's medium-term economic strategy and the need to ease the burden of adjustment at present falling on industry. Inflation has come down appreciably and is well below the current level of short-term interest rates.' An increase in employee national insurance contributions and a reported plan to increase the employers' share as well, increased criticism. Sir Geoffrey looked very beleaguered and isolated.

The Government had still more problems. By this time the North Sea was producing oil and Britain had become a net exporter of this essential fuel instead of an importer. When this development was combined with oil price increases and strict monetary policy, the country began to attract the attention of overseas investors. The value of the pound in foreign currencies rose rapidly and dramatically with the result that companies found it very difficult to export and firms, large and small, crashed into bankruptcy throwing tens of thousands of people out of work. It also forced the survivors to look for much greater efficiency.

Only economic historians and a few politicians probably now recall the shockwaves caused by the 1981 budget. The speech on 10 March 1981 contained the most direct repudiation of Keynesian economics there had been; deflationary at a time of recession and a total reverse of the conventional wisdom of post-war years. When a group of youngish, wettish Tory MPs met that evening they concluded that Howe's career was effectively over. 'Politics is the act of the possible. He was walking the plank. He was practising the art of the impossible,' a participant remembers today. However a colleague describes it as an absolute watershed. 'He had the courage to do exactly the opposite of what predecessors recommended and from that moment the recovery began.' Decisions, as is normal with Sir Geoffrey, were not reached lightly or quickly, with Treasury ministers, officials and advisers meeting for constant seminars to discuss papers and possibilities. Howe would also bounce ideas to and fro with friends.

In his paper, *Challenging Complacency*, Alan Walters said: 'The 1981 budget wrenched the Government deficit back onto its original course. This meant large increases in taxes – about £5 billion or more than two per cent of gross national product. The budget of 1981 must be reckoned as the biggest fiscal squeeze of peacetime. But it did convince the markets that the Government was going to stick to its policies. And, at first gradually, then much more rapidly, expectations adjusted to the reduced rates of inflation. Along this hard and rocky road, however, we were treated to an avalanche of protests by the massed ranks of the economics profession led by its most distinguished luminaries. It would have been so easy for the Government to ease up. But it would have been disastrous. In a trice all the progress that had been made in revising expectations would have been undone.'

Observing the Chancellor from the press gallery, Edward Pearce wrote: 'The odd thing about Geoffrey Howe is that although almost perversely mild and soft spoken (he does not just wear suede shoes, he talks in them), his wilfully grey manner conceals a taste in concrete policies for the dramatic. There is something endearing about his conjuror's ability to produce from a grey and battered hat a man-eating rabbit ... If you listened to Sir Geoffrey for his oratory you would hang yourself.

147

This man is absinthe masquerading as barley water. Like the good lawyer he is, Sir Geoffrey uses tedium like cuttlefish ink to obscure the news.' (*Looking Down on Mrs Thatcher*, published by Hamish Hamilton, 1987.)

For Howe, who instinctively sought consensus and agreement, the ferocity of opponents was wearying and worrying. Yet neither he nor Mrs Thatcher seemed to have any doubts about the propriety and urgency of sharp deflation. And Samuel Brittan, economics pundit and brother of Leon, who joined the Treasury as a minister in 1981, wrote in the *Financial Times*: 'The impression of tightening up by the abortive revolts of the Conservative MPs glorying in the name of "wets" and by the faster than predicted rise in unemployment was as important as the actual monetary fiscal mix.'

Nevertheless, 364 of the most august economists wrote a joint letter to the *Times* reflecting the establishment view that there was 'no basis in economic theory or supporting evidence for the Government's belief that by deflating demand they will bring inflation permanently under control.' It was an unprecedented attack, especially as economists are known for their inability to agree. However, within a few months inflation was falling even more rapidly than Treasury predictions. Monetarism became acceptable within the teaching cadres and the Keynesian hegemony was broken. The 1981 budget was a watershed in the history of economic theories as much as the fortunes of the Government.

By 1982 Geoffrey Howe had much more latitude in his budget. Government book-keeping was back on course and revenues from North Sea oil formed a new element of the state's finance. The rate of inflation was down fifteen per cent to seven per cent. Against that figure, even the closure of industry and rising unemployment seemed less important. With an ease which would not have been credible only three or four years earlier, the Chancellor, as unemployment passed the three million mark, said: 'Unemployment on this scale is here for a long time ... The scale is much larger than can be adjusted by government response. I think it is very important for the debate not to suggest that there is, lying around somewhere, some prescription or solution that, for some perverse reason, the Government is just putting on one side.'

But he hinted at the need for profound changes in funding obligations, which he would like to see the Government tackle. Unless the National Health Service and the welfare state could become more responsive to market forces, a fifty per cent rise in the basic rate of income tax to 45p in the pound and a twenty-five per cent VAT rate might be necessary. When a think-tank report setting out possible radical reforms of the welfare state was leaked just before the party conference that year, the subsequent uproar frightened the Government into abandoning change in this sector. Only after the 1987 election victory, the third in a row, did it find sufficient confidence to address the problems of financing and operating the NHS, and only then after enormous protests about staff shortages and ward closures. In 1982, Howe was also rehearsing the need to end mortgage tax relief arguing that its effect as a subsidy was merely to increase house prices and penalize the young. The married person's tax allowance was another target for reform as was relief on insurance policies. But prudence and the Prime Minister scotched these ideas.

By the time of the 1983 budget the party machine could blow its trumpet about the defeat of inflation (although it was bobbing along at five per cent which would have been regarded as scandalous in the 1950s). Geoffrey Howe had the pleasure of being able to tell Parliament: 'We have decisively broken the rising inflation trend that appeared so irresistible. We are now the first government for a quarter of a century to achieve a lower level of inflation than its predecessor.'

To go briefly through some of the events of this period can give only an impression of the breadth and depth of the changes introduced. Together with Mrs Thatcher he reset the compass for the ship that is Britain. On a personal and political level Geoffrey Howe, says a friend, came into his own and grew wings. In Opposition he had chaired the Treasury Policy Research Group, one of ninety-two policy groups set up by Keith Joseph, and published a list of more than fifty reforms which as Chancellor he steadily ploughed through. Much of his effort was concentrated on the containment of the un-glamorous borrowing requirement which he was convinced would lead to lower inflation and lower interest rates.

Another reform was the abolition of exchange control, which

for individuals saw the end to the property premium and the subsequent growth of second-home ownership, not simply by the rich. More important, it enabled companies and institutions to invest on a global scale which has already significantly affected the balance of payments and offers a totally different future than formerly anticipated for Britain, when the North Sea oil wells run dry. It also led to the huge expansion of the financial services sector and the development of the City of London, along with New York and Tokyo, as a world financial trading centre. At the time, when the results still lay in the uncertainty that is the future, it took tremendous courage. Against the advice of many Treasury and Bank of England officials, and the doubts of the Prime Minister, who said he would have to shoulder total responsibility for his action, Howe agonized and went ahead. Sometimes today he wears a tie with the Britannia crest and the notation EC 39–79. It was produced by the Bank to commemorate the occasion, which again, it should be said, led to major redundancies. It was, says a banker, the bravest thing he did and the most remarkable stroke of his Chancellorship.

In 1981 the Tory Party was well behind in the opinion polls. Although helpful, the decline in the rate of inflation was not the only factor which convinced the voters in the summer of 1983. Victory in the Falklands was undoubtedly a key factor. And while monetarism played a part in providing a sound basis for the more recent reduction in unemployment, its relaxation by Howe's successor at the Treasury, Nigel Lawson, when Howe moved on to the Foreign Office, and the consequent rise in money supply and demand set the scene for the 1987 election, when the Conservatives were returned for a third term.

15

Foreign Secretary

'Geoffrey is a thinker, writer and doer. When he starts in a job, there is nit-picking publicity and rude, personal, unnecessary stuff. He is said to be sleepy, if not actually accused of being thick. It starts like that and gradually it gets better. When things go wrong, a press officer may suggest you withdraw. That's counter-productive with Geoffrey. He is at his best. He doesn't retaliate in kind. But that doesn't mean he doesn't get hurt. He goes on with the usual business and tries to win the arguments, tries to persuade because that is democracy.'

This assessment by someone who knows him well certainly applies to his initiation as shadow Chancellor and to his early years at No 11 Downing Street, when flak flew about the increase in VAT; the consequent, if temporary, rise in inflation; the deepening recession in manufacturing; and rising unemployment, before any of the real rewards of policy changes began to emerge. It equally applied when he moved from No 11 to the Foreign Office in the summer of 1983 and had to attempt to disentangle national egos in negotiations over competing needs, wishes and ideals. In this respect, there may be significance that at the end of 1987 the most obvious ornament in his office was a heavy bronze troika with tense driver controlling and directing highly strung horses on a single path. The impressive and beautiful object also happens to be

151

a present from Eduard Shevardnadze, his opposite number in the Soviet Union and crucial player in the continuous struggle for power – and peace.

On the wall opposite Sir Geoffrey's desk hangs a massive portrait of Lord Palmerston, the anti-democratic but liberal Tory who spent nearly twenty years as Secretary at War, enjoyed three long spells in the Foreign Office, moved on to the Home Office and then became Prime Minister from 1859 until 1865, when he died. He was eighty-one. So much for early retirement, with men and women of fifty now asked to make way for youth. But then Sir Geoffrey, who has passed his sixtieth birthday, still thinks of himself as quite a young man. He also has an inordinate ability to weather political and personal storms like some well-balanced buoy, which remains upright whatever the height, strength and power of the waves. 'He does not seem to show stress,' says one colleague. 'If anything, he gets more analytical as the problem or crisis intensifies.' Although he can display flashes of anger at unnecessary incompetence or sloppy thinking, his temper lies at the end of a very long fuse and he never panics – or, if he does, nobody knows.

Certainly Sir Geoffrey's composure, general amiability and confidence must all have been sorely tested at times as he moved into the Foreign Office and began to superimpose his strategy and tactics on the works of generations of forebears. Hardly had he started meeting world leaders on their home ground and getting to grips with detail than he was embroiled in the United States' invasion of Grenada, the ban on union membership at Government Communications Headquarters Cheltenham (GCHQ), and, although the European Community was familiar territory, an almost unholy row over the budget, agriculture and Britain's rebate. In the House of Commons the going was very rough indeed.

On 17 October 1983 a coup overturned the Government of Grenada. Maurice Bishop, Prime Minister and leader of the People's Revolutionary Government, was arrested by a rival faction headed by his deputy prime minister and the commander of the armed forces. A crowd of 3,000 marched on the barracks where he and others were interned and he was killed. Although the Governor General, Sir Paul Scoon, was requesting foreign assistance and the United States was concerned about the numbers of Cubans employed in the construction of a new international airport and the safety of its nationals, Sir Geoffrey assured the House of Commons that neither the United States nor the United Kingdom had invasion plans. On 25 October about 400 marines and 1,500 paratroops took part in 'Urgent Fury', bombed a hospital for the mentally ill and brought the island under control within two days. The British Foreign Secretary called for their withdrawal. It was not the happiest time in Anglo-American understanding but Margaret Thatcher as Prime Minister at least had the pleasure and relief of saying precisely what she thought: 'If you are going to pronounce a new law that wherever Communism runs against the will of the people the United States shall enter, then we are going to have really terrible wars in the world.'

The Americans handed over control to soldiers and police from other parts of the Caribbean and within two months their troops had gone. But the whole affair left a nasty aftertaste of ignorance, official incompetence and cavalier treatment by the Americans.

In little more than a month, GCHQ was back in the news and Sir Geoffrey was lumbered, against his own deep-seated convictions, with a public image as repressor of human rights. Because of the special nature of the work of this secretive organization as it listens, looks and analyses flows of information relating to defence and foreign policy, the Government announced a ban on normal trade union membership. Employees were to be paid £1,000 outright for withdrawal of previous rights, transferred to less sensitive jobs elsewhere or allowed to opt for retirement. The decision basically stemmed from the conviction of Geoffrey Prime on charges under the Official Secrets Act in 1982 and the subsequent Security Commission report, which recommended amongst other things: wider staff searches, more radical screening and a pilot use of a lie detector. However the ban was in fact introduced to prevent strikes in an organization which keeps twenty-four-hour watch for 365 days a year. Reaction was immediate and prolonged with pandemonium in the House of Commons after it emerged that some members of GCHQ staff might be dismissed. Sir Geoffrey's handling was described as shambolic. Neil Kinnock, leader of the Labour Party, attacked him for 'calculated victimization' and 'despotism'; David Owen, Leader of the Social Democratic Party, said he should consider resignation. There was a half-day strike in parts of the civil service and the Trades Union Congress decided to shun meetings of the National Economic Development Council and to go to law, at first with success. In July, the High Court ruled that the Government's action was invalid and of no effect. In August, the Court of Appeal overturned this verdict and in November the House of Lords upheld the Appeal Court saying that the Government's action was justified on grounds of national security.

As Terry Coleman wrote in the *Guardian* in April 1987, James Callaghan, former Labour Prime Minister and now a member of the House of Lords, soon learnt when he became a junior minister 'when in trouble in the House keep your head down, speak in a monotone, don't look up if you can help it, and be as uninteresting as possible'. Sir Geoffrey is a natural for this approach and he plodded relentlessly on, his voice low, his manner mild, his sentences long as he wore down the edge of political attack. While the fury subsided, his image in many parts of the press increasingly became that of a waffler; Margaret Thatcher's poodle, friendly but malleable.

At much the same time however some of the endless negotiations which go on between countries over long-standing problems were beginning to show light. He had taken a grip of issues and a number were beginning to reflect his views and ability to shape official thinking.

The members of the European Community had been wrangling over the new budget for months, with Mrs Thatcher so living up to her reputation as the Iron Lady that the Greek Prime Minister, Andreas Papandreou, after the Brussels meeting, said he felt that the other partners would be greatly relieved if Britain left. However, in June 1984, the European Community reached a historic agreement at Fontainebleau on a new, bigger but tighter budget with an agreed rebate for the United Kingdom. Britain was to get more of its money back and a major crisis had passed. Both Margaret Thatcher and Geoffrey Howe made crucial contributions.

The second event, which heralded a new sense of purpose, was the Hong Kong agreement which, although signed by the Prime Minister, was very much Sir Geoffrey's personal responsibility. Under the 1898 treaty, the New Territories were and are due to be returned to China in 1997, and the British Government had the delicate task of negotiating an agreement to guarantee the safety, prosperity and freedom of its 5,300,000 inhabitants – ninety-eight per cent of whom have Chinese origins. Following Mrs Thatcher's visit in September 1982, talks started on talks; in other words on procedure not content. Apart from honouring the treaty, there was absolutely no question of any declaration of independence – for one thing Hong Kong's water supply comes from the mainland – and Britain had to find a way of ensuring that the return to Chinese control would not kill the thriving economic goose and its ability to lay golden eggs.

When Sir Geoffrey became Foreign Secretary, the totally confidential talks, led by the British Ambassador to Peking Richard Evans, now Sir Richard, had not advanced very far. The British had two main cards – the importance of Hong Kong to China as a source of foreign exchange, and its potential role as a prototype, but only if the transfer was and is successful, for any long-term reunification with Taiwan. Sir Geoffrey made two visits at crunch points in the negotiations and very much took control, building up a personal relationship of trust with his opposite number, Wu Xueqian, and guiding officials in detailed tactics so that concessions made and accepted remained part of the original overall design. The Chinese have their own negotiating techniques and part of the problem was that the British never knew precisely what the arrangements for a meeting would be or who would be there. If a meeting went well, the negotiations would open up to the next political tier but there was always the fear that if one card too many was played, the whole process would collapse.

Language and ideology also created barriers; the British trying to impress on the Chinese the fragility of confidence in a capitalist system, and the Chinese unable to understand that even if they had promises from key countries about their continued support, they would be meaningless in this context. Governments do not invest. If confidence evaporated, so would investment and investors. Communications and comprehension were as difficult as persuading the colour-blind that green is in reality red. Eventually, Sir Geoffrey developed his own metaphors and described Hong Kong as a delicate precious Ming vase which had to be kept intact and unharmed in the great relay race as the British passed the responsibility over to their Chinese team-mates. This vase was endowed with magnets which attracted capital and the essential thing was to keep it as an entity if it was to carry on as before. At such times, years of advocacy can come into their own. As former Lord Chancellor and Cabinet colleague Lord Hailsham says: 'Lawyers have had experience with difficult judges who have the power of deciding against you but still need to be educated as to the strength of your case. It needs patience, dedication and persistence. Geoffrey has persistence, courage and integrity. The advocate's training does assist you in negotiations. Many cases have to be settled and some cases have to be won against initially adverse tribunals. People pay for your opinions, not your doubts, but the lawyer's weakness is that he sometimes finds it difficult to make up his mind on things which demand an instant decision.'

After painstaking progress, the joint agreement was initialled in September 1984 and formally signed in the Great Hall of the People in Beijing on 19 December 1984. It allows for the creation of Hong Kong as a special administrative region with a high degree of autonomy except in foreign affairs and defence; its own form of local government and independent judiciary; and the maintenance of private property combined with social and economic freedom. As Chairman Deng Xiaoping finally summarized the conclusion of the negotiations with extraordinary but apt simplicity: 'One country. Two systems.'

Sir Geoffrey was to emphasize a number of aspects relating to the Hong Kong negotiations almost one year later when he spoke to the Royal College of Defence Studies in London about his first two and a half years in the Foreign Office. 'It is astonishing how the key to a negotiation can be found in four words like that – one country, China, two systems, communism and capitalism. Once you are taught the value of a four words slogan of that kind you find yourself using the same technique on far too many occasions. At the end of that

156

particularly long set of negotiations and the banquet that closed the proceedings I was able to say that we had started at the beginning as we had, with eleven a side on the negotiating table, not certain whether we were going to play football or cricket, but at the conclusion of the proceedings, having arrived at our accord, we could regard ourselves as two teams, one goal, which is the sort of language you can use.'

Sir Geoffrey also related an anecdote which again gives something of the flavour of his approach to people and ambience. With more than a hint of the inscrutability so often attributed to the Chinese, he recalled asking their Foreign Minister, at a dinner, about the history of a particularly impressive candelabra. To the reply that it was not more than 300 years old, Sir Geoffrey remarked that, if either of them had been American, they would both have said: 'Do you realize this candelabra is well over 250 years old.' But both of them, he added, belonged to mature peoples with a long history and were able to understand the insight of not more than 300 years old. That is not small talk, but flattery, friendship, understanding and equality wrapped up in a few well chosen words.

The British Foreign Secretary is quite adept at breaking the ice. On a visit to Zambia in 1985, peals of laughter erupted from President Kaunda after a somewhat nervous start to a working breakfast. It emerged later that Sir Geoffrey had somehow started telling the story about a person who had died and was asking the Archangel Gabriel at the entrance to heaven: 'What's God like?' and received the answer: 'Well, for a start, she's black.' On another occasion, at a European Community meeting which had reached a sticky point, with one minister switching an argument back to front, the Foreign Secretary recalled an advertisement from his childhood of a pig pulling a trolley piled high with sausages and the suggestion that he was drawing his own conclusion. When he gently made the comparison with the minister's argument, everyone convulsed into laughter and the tension snapped. His humour tends however to be restricted to small groups, not Parliament or larger audiences.

The speech to the Royal College of Defence Studies was unusual in that, instead of concentrating on policy, he gave an account of the way he thinks and works. In particular he drew lessons from his negotiations with the Chinese. Hong Kong, he said, using a Chinese phrase, was a problem left over from history, as were Gibraltar and Northern Ireland. 'To be confronted with the conundrum of one of the world's most thriving capitalist economies on territory that at the end of twelve years from now reverts to one of the world's leading Communist governments was to face a conundrum indeed,' he said.

Whatever and wherever the negotiations, it was generally possible, he said, to identify 'a hurdle of comprehension', which had to be overcome if the negotiations were to succeed, although in Europe the hurdle was more like an infinitely high mountain with a series of false summits. The real hurdle in Brussels had been to secure the perception of the need for a rational foundation. With Hong Kong the most formidable hurdle was to convince the Chinese leadership of British sincerity and trust. In Ireland it had been the legitimacy of the wishes of the majority of the people of Northern Ireland, in East–West discussions 'the mountain of mutual balanced suspicion' and the need of the Soviet Union and the United States to convince each other they were earnest in their search for better management.

'A lot of diplomacy is not about solving problems but about managing them,' he went on. 'A lot of diplomacy is like matrimonial relations at their worst in which your task, confronted with a row about who does the washing up, is to bring that row to a conclusion in the knowledge that you are going to have to go on living with each other for the rest of time. In matrimonial relations there is always the prospect of a divorce. There is no prospect of a divorce between East and West and so the parties are destined to live with each other in an arranged marriage where they have no choice as to their partner. And in that, to have achieved a way of managing the situation is to have achieved something worthwhile.'

So far as negotiation techniques were concerned, Sir Geoffrey emphasized the need to define aims realistically without illusion; to have clear insight into one's priorities; to recognize that negotiations were in part a bilateral process of education; and to establish a set of consistent reliable signals so that 'you know what you mean when you say something, so that when you say for example this for me is a fundamental point of principle, the chap on the other side of the table knows whether that means what it says or not'. (In other words, Whitehall speke writ international.) Personal chemistry undoubtedly played some part, he added. 'I find that in a sense the most humbling thing of all; that relations for a decade, a century, between two great nations, in our case of more than 50 million people and in the Chinese case of more than a billion people, that the actual management of those relations do depend to an extent upon the personal chemistry of my relationship with my Chinese opposite number,' he said.

16

Strategy and Tactics

While the Foreign Secretary could talk about his approach – the arranged marriages between countries; the management of problems left by history; dialogue and the need for clear assessment of priorities – he could not of course say how others see him. Sir Geoffrey's stamina is now legendary, as is his need to explore every alternative alley, cul-de-sac, road, street, drive and avenue of policy before making up his mind. He will ask for more submissions and then yet more, savouring detail as well as salving a legal neurosis to cover every eventuality and angle before working out how best to present or tackle a case. He will amend and alter policy documents again and again. The same is equally true of drafts of major speeches which will be more and more finely tuned in hours of round-table sessions. The process does not make for speedy decisions, which is the only criticism generally voiced, apart from low-key presentation including over-slow exposition in Cabinet. ('Speak up, Geoffrey. We haven't got all day,' might be the *Spitting Image* take-off.) But the process also leads to innovation as he rearranges blocks of information and ideas relating to the apparently insoluble and comes up with a potentially more fruitful new approach.

His private office is headed by his principal private secretary, who looks after co-ordination, security and policy and accompanies him on nearly all trips except some day returns into mainland Europe. It is a job for high-fliers. Brian Fall went on to become Lord Carrington's chef du cabinet in NATO and is now senior minister in Washington. Len Appleyard, who first held this role working for Sir Geoffrey, is now British Ambassador to Hungary. Tony Galsworthy, the subsequent incumbent, took part in the Hong Kong negotiations. Next come two assistant private secretaries, who split the world; another assistant private secretary who manages the Foreign Secretary's diary; two special political advisers; another assistant private secretary who heads up the registry (in other words, files and information); and a number of clerical officers and secretaries, not to mention his driver and police security.

For the principal private secretary, at least, the normal working day starts at 8 am and finishes at 9 pm, when up to three black boxes are locked and delivered to Sir Geoffrey for overnight home work. There may be twelve inches of paper – submissions on key problems in the form of highly compressed information and argument plus perhaps ten per cent or some 200 of the telegrams recording communications between Whitehall and British outposts all over the world. By 8.15 am at the latest the boxes are back in the office, the papers annotated in red ink. It is a spidery hand which sometimes squiggles to one side when the Foreign Secretary has temporarily nodded off in the dark early hours. He really does work when others sleep and his office is hard put to keep up with the one man's constant flow of papers, energy and ideas. They do not see much of family or friends.

However, although enormously demanding, Sir Geoffrey inspires genuine devotion among those in his immediate entourage and the real affection of staff such as messengers and doormen whom he treats quite simply as equals. In the Foreign Office he is sometimes known as Sir Geoff, as he was once repeatedly called on a visit to Zimbabwe. And there is even a plaque in India dedicated to Sir Geoferely. While instinctively liked by most people, he is less beloved by some, who are a little resentful that, because of his own capacity for endless hard work, he creates unnecessary extra toil for others. There is too the perhaps inevitable jealousy of the school swot, who has carried on swotting and demonstrably proved the effort pays off. He has after all held four major offices of state including Chancellor of the Exchequer, when the classicist took on board economics. More recently, as Foreign Secretary, the problems of peace, defence, terrorism, arms control, famine, Third World development and trade have all been absorbed.

Sir Geoffrey simply never stops. If reading matter is exhausted on a long flight, the private secretary who sits alongside can expect to fill a notebook with a varied selection of Hovian thoughts on which to act on arrival and when they return to headquarters in King Charles II Street. Normally the group travels on longer hauls by special VC10 and a Hawker Siddeley 125 executive jet into mainland Europe. According to the length of trip, his entourage will comprise one or two private secretaries; a couple of specialist departmental advisers; the head of news; a detective; support staff and, quite frequently, Lady Howe.

A working ambience of cheerful good humour and people is important and he regularly sounds out his private secretaries. But if Sir Geoffrey is ever ready to debate and open to ideas, delegation is quite a different matter. He is painstaking in his briefing and preparation for meetings. If a subject is at all complicated, he will commit his brief to memory the night before and then enter the session armed with clutch cards containing perhaps two or three sentences as personal autocues. For the European Council of foreign ministers he will also carry a further eleven cards with notes of individual points he wishes to raise with each colleague during the course of the visit. Sir Geoffrey will have read voluminous papers, which they quite happily and perhaps sensibly leave to one side, and he will enjoy dropping into the discussion some apposite fact or quotation. His colleagues, with whom he is popular, are suitably impressed.

The British Foreign Secretary, according to people close to his office, never forgets his overall aims and objectives – in other words he manages to see the wood as well as the trees. He is also constantly aware of other people's goals and problems in any negotiations and tries to find ways for them to reach a satisfactory conclusion as well. While Sir Geoffrey is slow to reveal and play his cards, if he can so lead a conversation that his opposite number proposes what he already had in mind, so much the better. 'He is always looking for a way to allow the chap to reach the conclusion of his own accord,' a Foreign Office official comments. It is generally held that Sir Geoffrey is patient, persistent, never deterred by failure, ever-optimistic and even sometimes a little naive or childlike in his belief that people of good faith, including Margaret Thatcher, will see things his way in the end because reason is on his side. One former associate tried to sum up this obviously complex man by suggesting that his character displays elements of Puck, Socrates, Father Brown, Dr Dolittle and Pooh Bear.

The Foreign Office is not too worried if there are times when he soothes people into sleep. Lack of drama can be a definite advantage in defusing over-emotional and potentially dangerous situations, while his imperturbability acts as shield against the slings and arrows of both the outraged and outrageous. In the House of Commons he regularly negotiates the minefield of parliamentary questions, making good use of his phenomenal memory and his ability to run the words through the computer which is his brain before they reach his lips.

Sir Geoffrey's miserable trail around the rulers of South Africa in the summer of 1986 suffering vindictive abuse from both black and white leaders, including public castigation by President Kaunda in front of the television cameras of the world, is described as 'a sort of personal Calvary'. While it is normal practice in Zambia to have newsmen in for the first part of a private meeting, which is bound to result in a well-calculated performance from the leader, it is not so normal to hound a visitor to the point where many people would simply have stalked out in cold or hot fury. That course is believed to have entered Sir Geoffrey's mind too – but he decided, as he did as a boxer in army training, that, whatever the battering, he'd stay in the ring.

In South Africa his sessions with President Botha, even if held in total privacy, were said to be equally bad-tempered which certainly helped keep up staff morale. After all, if both black and white Africa were so fractious, the policy must at least be balanced. 'If there is a chance that representatives of the free world can nudge the wheel of history towards peace and reconciliation in South Africa, then that chance must surely be seized,' Sir Geoffrey told the press after one of his sessions in Pretoria. 'That is the central purpose of my mission on behalf of the twelve countries of the European Community. I represent not just twelve governments, but values that have been forged in the fires of two world wars: reconciliation, not conflict; consent, not coercion; justice and freedom, not domination. To discover, as a conciliator, that my mission is viewed with mingled doubt, suspicion or even hostility on many sides, does not discourage me. If it were not so, there would be no problems between those who want more change and those who resist it. All I can say to every side is that talking can solve many problems however difficult, and violence few.' If the trip was a diplomatic failure, in that it did not achieve the hopeless, he personally returned with his reputation enhanced. Nowadays, as well as being a major reforming Chancellor, it is suggested he is likely to prove at least one of the best Foreign Secretaries since the Second World War.

While their presentation of the argument will differ, both he and the Prime Minister genuinely share their revulsion for apartheid and their distrust of sanctions. 'Apartheid is not only morally abhorrent, it is in practical terms untenable and incompatible with economic dynamics,' Sir Geoffrey said in a speech at the Royal Commonwealth Society in London towards the end of 1983. 'The demand for black workers, the increase in their purchasing power, the development of black trade unions – all give impetus to a powerful dynamo for change inside South African society. To allow the dogma of apartheid to block the benign forces of the market place would be to the benefit of no one.'

While economic forces offered some hope that the evils of apartheid could be moderated, he continued, political reform was also necessary. Britain would reaffirm the Government's commitment to the Gleneagles Agreement on apartheid in sport; it would uphold the United Nations arms embargo; eschew any military collaboration with Africa, and not help the country with its nuclear programme. 'But we are not going to cut off contact with South Africa,' he said. 'You can only influence someone if you are ready to talk to him. You cannot get your point across by refusing even to discuss your differences.' And later: 'Equally we do not think that the case has been made for economic sanctions against South Africa. Positive change in South Africa is likely to come about through a growth in contact with the rest of the world, not by treating it as a pariah. And through development of its economy, not by the imposition of a commercial siege. If the black states and South Africa want to influence one another, they must talk to each other, express their concerns and explain the constraints under which they work. Nothing can or will be solved in an atmosphere of isolation and mutual suspicion.'

In July 1985 he was back on the same stage and the same subject. 'Apartheid is unacceptable, unworkable and indefensible ... contrary to all British and Commonwealth values ... given added repugnance by the existence side by side of two communities – a ruling minority and a majority deprived of power – between whom the inequalities, in terms of material possessions, education and expectations are vast. Most repugnant of all is the fact that these inequalities are built upon foundations of racial discrimination,' he said. Unlike many British people, colour does not really register with Sir Geoffrey. Since his national service in Kenya, he has been completely at ease with all races and believes the world one great melting pot in which differences are bound gradually to become blurred.

'Our differences are about means rather than ends,' he continued in his 1985 Royal Commonwealth Society speech. 'We oppose sanctions because we believe that economic growth in South Africa offers the most likely route for peaceful political change. We should be looking for ways of strengthening these internal economic forces, especially the growing economic power of the black community, the black trade union movement and the facilities for training and education of blacks. The application of sanctions would mean an end to all these activities ... The most urgent priority is action and action of a convincing and effective kind, to create a climate of confidence which will permit a real dialogue with the genuine leaders of the black community whom blacks must be permitted to choose. The dialogue cannot avoid the fundamental question of the political aspiration of blacks. And the dialogue must be seriously meant and tenaciously pursued. This requires bold steps by the South African Government – the

165

unconditional release of Nelson Mandela and other acknowledged political leaders; an end to forced removals; an end
to detention without trial; an early end to the State of Emergency; the progressive abolition of discriminatory legislation
such as the pass laws and the Group Areas Act; a commitment
to some form of common citizenship for all South Africans.
I am sure that all those who are working for peaceful evolutionary change in South Africa know that an outcome must be
found whereby white South Africans are guaranteed their
rightful place, but not more than their rightful place, in any
future South African political system ... The private sector
must continue challenging these conditions (apartheid), which
impede its own success as much as they are socially unjust
... There is considerable scope for further initiative by British
companies: community works, social welfare of their
employees, equal opportunities. And the private sector must
play a full part in the broader political life of South Africa,
condemning repression and working for peaceful change.'

'Peace,' he told the Conservative Party conference in
October 1985, 'can be secured by the force of persuasion but
not by the persuasion of force.'

17

Security and Prosperity

The relationship of any Foreign Secretary with No 10 Downing Street carries inbuilt tension and rivalry. The nature of the job creates an independent, high-profile role in all four quarters of the globe yet, when the great occasion arrives, be it treaty signing or meetings of the super powers, the Prime Minister takes pride of place. For all the reports of rows between Sir Geoffrey and Margaret Thatcher, he simply shrugs off their importance saying that most marriages have broken up in less time than they have worked closely together. He is supremely loyal, patient, ready to provide a pillar of strength and yield the limelight, as he did on her much heralded trip to Moscow.

However her instant star appeal and obvious Boadicean strength can cause problems to those who judge simply by appearances and underestimate the steel inside the amiable exterior. In Japan early in 1988, Sir Geoffrey was introduced as 'the soft wife of the Iron Lady'. Whatever precision may have been lost in translation, few men would relish such a backhanded compliment. The Foreign Secretary simply replied that there was no question about his sex and he would prefer to be known as the 'robust partner', which he undoubtedly is. Particularly in Europe, where both are fully conversant with Common Market intricacies and technicalities, they make a formidable team. On a good day, they are reportedly lethal. 'Not only does she express herself with extreme cogency and knows the details but he knows even more and is master of the art of community politics,' says a home town supporter. 'Once they get into their stride, there is no other European country which can withstand them.' But that of course does not mean they have it all their own way. There was a particularly sticky period, when the Americans bombed Libya with British agreement, about the use of aircraft based in this country and Sir Geoffrey gave no advance warning to the Council of Foreign Ministers at the meeting which just preceded the raid.

The Prime Minister has had her special relationships, especially President Ronald Reagan and Soviet leader Mikhail Gorbachev; Sir Geoffrey has his in China, Europe and the Commonwealth. Their styles are very different, their approach to most areas of policy, excepting perhaps the Falklands and Gibraltar, remarkably similar. Mrs Thatcher will however react with a 'No, because', whereas Sir Geoffrey may seem to placate with a 'Yes, but'. Nobody can be nasty to the Foreign Secretary, who is much more instinctively at home in Europe and can psychologically play his known reasonableness to good effect against the proven stickiness, if not spikiness, of his partner. The downside to this 'rolling-pin factor' is the need for some leaders to have to prove they can survive three rounds in the ring and still be standing.

On this basis Sir Geoffrey has now stood his ground since 1975. There is one story of a former Cabinet colleague who said: 'It's terrible the way Geoffrey lets Margaret just shout and shout' and the perceptive rejoinder: 'He's like a tank going through a river. He goes straight through the torrent and roaring water, up the bank and straight on where he intended to go.' A former Tory MP says that dealing with the Prime Minister is like going over the top in the First World War, the danger being that other ministers will lose their independence of thought and simply follow her lead or, if they do not cave in, they go. 'Geoffrey Howe,' he said using a similar illustration, 'has the ability to shut the lid, close down the vehicle, go under the water and emerge the other side perhaps dripping but with essential elements of his position intact.' Told to shut up, he is said quietly to insist: 'No, Prime Minister. This is an important point.' Unlike some ministers, who no longer hold office, he is totally loyal and does not tell tales out of school. Mrs Thatcher respects his understanding of issues and grasp of detail and there have been times like the Westland affair when she has needed his solid support.

He has an advantage over many men of his education and generation in that he genuinely admires women and enjoys working with them. Lady Howe may have been deputy chairman of the Equal Opportunities Commission and he may query the shortage of senior women in the Foreign Office but Sir Geoffrey spoke up for women even in the monastic environment of war-time Winchester. He listens to women and co-operates but does what he wants as well.

His constant short breaks in the countries of the world can give the impression of excessive zeal, energy and perhaps a childlike enjoyment of formal occasions and the chance to see a few wonders of the world. In 1986 he travelled some 143,000 air and sea miles, and in 1987 117,000, which was still more than 300 miles for every day of the year, despite time spent on the hustings during the General Election. However, with his normal red-carpet VIP treatment, he can make personal contact with most people who matter in a mere three days and returns therefore better able to weigh up the constant barrage of reports and advice which daily cross his desk. He has also begun or continued to build up personal relationships which can be crucial where negotiations depend on trust.

While generally accepted that his personal achievements include Hong Kong (his particular monument), Gibraltar, improved British credentials and standing in Europe and, with Mrs Thatcher, helping to keep arms talks between the United States and the Soviet Union on an even keel, the Foreign Office rates his speech on 'star wars' or President Reagan's strategic defence initiative as his most striking and pathfinding contribution so far. In March 1985 Sir Geoffrey's quiet words caused political furore in house with the Whitehall grapevine whispering that the Prime Minister was very angry indeed. However, internationally it upgraded him from mere politician to statesman. He had opened up for debate the very far-reaching consequences of the possible adoption of active defence, possibly in space, against ballistic missiles after forty years in which both West and East had successfully relied on deterrence. Like

169

most of his speeches, the language is simple and the text closely argued, the whole being undoubtedly better than its parts. He does not seem able to produce the simple summary, the three paragraphs, in graphic if not purple prose, which instantly make the news.

At the Royal United Services Institute in London he basically questioned the future nature of western strategy, how best to enhance deterrence and to curb rather than stimulate a new arms race. 'The history of weapons development and the strategic balance shows only too clearly that research into new weapons and study of their strategic implications must go hand in hand,' Sir Geoffrey told his audience. 'Otherwise research may acquire an unstoppable momentum of its own, even though the case for stopping may strengthen with the passage of years. We must take care that political decisions are not pre-empted by the march of technology, still less by premature attempts to predict the route of that march.'

While accepting the need to match similar research in the eastern bloc, he then raised a number of questions. How far could the risks be offset of switching from mutual deterrence to a possibly limited active defence against weapons of devastating destructive force? Might the active defence of key installations be viewed as fostering an aggressive policy? Would it increase the threat to civilians by stimulating a return to the targeting policies of the 1950s? Would the supposed technology work, survive and prove cost-effective? 'There would be no advantage in creating a new Maginot Line of the twenty-first century, liable to be outflanked by relatively simpler and demonstrably cheaper counter-measures,' he went on. 'If the technology does work, what will be the psychological impact on the other side? ... If the ballastic missile showed signs of becoming impotent and obsolete, how would protection be extended against the non-ballistic nuclear threat, the threat posed by aircraft or cruise missiles, battlefield nuclear weapons or, in the last resort, by covert action? What other defences, in addition to space-based systems, would need to be developed and at what cost, to meet these continuing threats? ... Could we be certain that the new system would permit adequate political control over both nuclear weapons and defensive systems, or might we find ourselves in a situation where the peace of the world rested solely upon computers and automatic decision-making?'

Apart from cost, there were also implications for arms control and the danger that the prospect of new defences would inexorably crank up the levels of the offensive nuclear systems they were designed to overwhelm. 'The fact that there are no easy answers, that the risks may outweigh the benefits, that science may not be able to provide a safer solution to the nuclear dilemma of the past forty years than we have found already – all these points underline the importance of proceeding with the utmost deliberation,' he warned. That speech, which originally infuriated right-wing Americans, has now become part of the thinking man's orthodoxy.

Sir Geoffrey enjoys using speeches to expound and expand his thinking and that therefore of the British Government on areas of policy, and months in advance he plans themed topics for selected, major speaking platforms in his diary. In 1984 and 1985 five speeches were delivered in Bonn, Berlin, Milan, Paris and The Hague and subsequently published under the title *Europe Tomorrow*. More recently, a series of four, given in London (two), Brussels and Chicago, covered East–West relations. It too was published.

Europe Tomorrow provides a positive dossier on Britain's attitudes on everything from food mountains and the Common Agricultural Policy to community institutions; continuing obstacles to free trade and peace. As he has said: 'Ministers and officials criss-crossing Europe to haggle over ice-cream labelling are not a glamorous sight. But governments so engaged are not governments preparing to fight each other. After centuries of war and poverty in Europe this is, to put it mildly, no bad thing. The price of peace is eternal vigilance – but the value of peace is that it allows us to dwell on the ordinary things in life.'

The removal of trade, travel and other barriers within Europe very much fits in with his passionate belief in the virtues of free markets and their essential role in the promotion of prosperity. He is also convinced, as he wrote in *Crossbow* in the autumn of 1984, that in a world of multilateral diplomacy and alliances, the European Community is for Britain the most effective setting in which to bring its influence to bear. 'It is in Europe that our national security and political and economic interests are most directly and continuously engaged,' he said in an essay on British foreign policy. 'It is in Europe that British ministers, if we are ready to sustain the initiative, can work most effectively for British prosperity and for world peace.' The Government's foreign policy was based, he stated, on awareness of the need for domestic strength to underpin Britain's efforts abroad, a belief in Britain as a country with a future as well as a past, and a realistic assessment of the international environment.

Certainly his speech series on Europe confirmed that Britain, even if it had opted out of the early years, now had no doubt about its role as one of the leading members. 'We brought to Europe a considerable dowry: our markets for agricultural and industrial goods, our fishing grounds, our major contribution to the defence and security of our continent,' he said in Bonn. 'It is because we have so much at stake in the community, because we depend so much on its healthy development and because we believe so wholeheartedly in its future that we have devoted so much effort to the reform of its internal arrangements; to building a better foundation for the future of Europe.'

In Berlin: the European Community is 'constructive not defensive. It is about collective strength, not individual power. It aims not to promote the interest of one member state but of all and in so doing to strengthen the free institutions of all western countries ... Many other traditional sources of conflict are still with us ... What has changed is the way we tackle these problems among ourselves in Europe. We no longer do it through old-fashioned power politics, with the ultimate threat of resort to arms. Instead we sit around the council table in Brussels and Luxembourg, searching for solutions through reasoned arguments and compromise. Vigorously and heatedly, perhaps, but always peacefully.'

In Milan: 'Frontier formalities can be made less complicated and less costly. All Europeans should be working to ensure that insurance services, for example, can be bought and sold freely between all community countries, just like manufactured goods. I also look forward to the day when the stock markets of Europe become more closely integrated ... The European market must be free of internal barriers ... In research and development, where costs in the field of high technology have become very high, we must work together ... We must tackle the excesses of agricultural expenditure which absorb over seventy per cent of the total community budget.'

In Paris: 'We want to take this habit of co-operation further into all possible fields, particularly those areas at the cutting edge of the new technology. The civilian use of space is one obvious example ... For some people these may still seem remote, fantastic visions. I disagree. They may be tomorrow's problems. But if we don't start to tackle tomorrow's problems today, Europe will soon be living on its yesterdays.'

And at The Hague: 'There is a better way to solve Europe's problems than by the use of force and counterforce. We have shown in the West that the disputes of centuries can be peacefully solved and transcended. We have respected the sovereignty of states – whatever short-term complications and inhibitions it may bring ... We must set out to apply the same principles consistently to East–West problems as well ... What we want is to keep a better future open for Europe: for both parts of Europe, and for every man and woman in them. A freer future in every sense: including freedom from the burden and tension of the present "armed peace" in Europe.'

'Europe should be, I believe will be, an economic superpower,' he told the London School of Economics Conservative Association in 1986. 'And, if we can keep improving our co-operation on foreign policy, a political giant too, with Britain playing a mainstream role.'

It is the British, he emphasizes, who are pressing for the dismantling of air cartels, the freeing of financial services, the harmonization of new technological standards and the wider use of the Ecu; whereas other countries persist in keeping exchange controls and cramp Europe's insurance markets. He finds it slightly strange that the British should be quite so protective about blue passports which were only introduced in 1920. He has also flirted with the concept of voluntary identity cards, common in the rest of Europe, as an important aid to the control of terrorism, illegal immigration and social service frauds. Birth certificates, which have to be shown from time to time, are already a form of official identity, he says. And, as for the Channel Tunnel, it will provide for the first time an internal land frontier. 'Would we, could we, still maintain the full panoply of external customs controls at our end of the link, with every lorry and motor car stopped and checked, that we do today?' the Foreign Secretary asked in Edinburgh. 'Would we remain insular and defensive – revelling in controls barely less than three-quarters of a century old?'

According to Christopher Tugendhat, the former European budget commissioner who is chairman of the Civil Aviation Authority, Sir Geoffrey 'played an indispensable role in seeing through the British budget dispute and getting it settled. He has managed to get people to come away from rhetorical generalisations to facing up to the tasks that actually have to be done. He is listened to because he has something to say, not just of what is of immediate British interest but also something relevant to the concerns of others.'

Outside as well as inside Europe, the British Foreign Secretary is equally adamant in his anti-protectionist stance. In 1987 he told an audience in Chicago that freedom, democracy and justice faced two challenges – the threat to prosperity posed from within by economic mismanagement, most notably by the forces of protectionism, and the threat to security posed from without by the Soviet Union and its Communist allies. The key to Britain's growth and rapidly advancing prosperity had been found 'not in retreating behind trade barriers, but in taking them down'. Sir Geoffrey went on: 'We have not closed our economy, but opened it. This has been our sure path to success. This success means good business for you as well as for us. Britain is now the largest direct investor in the United States and America the largest direct investor in Britain. The European Community is the largest world market for American exports and vice versa . . . Contrast the advantage of an open trading system such as ours with the closed, centrally planned economies of the Soviet bloc. Almost forty years after they turned their backs on the offer of American Marshall Aid, most Eastern European countries are still living with the kind of economic deprivation which most Western European countries had left behind them by the 1950s. Food rationing and chronic power shortages are still common.'

He may have delivered his opinions with his usual soft-spoken courtesy but the Foreign Secretary was perfectly prepared to criticize his hosts. 'If we are to lighten the debt burden on the poorer countries, then we need to restrain our own demand for scarce capital. That is the only way to keep down the cost of borrowing. This is why the world has, for some years now, watched with mounting dismay as your country, the richest in the world, has become the world's largest importer of capital. For in this way the formidable federal deficit has doubly damaged the free world economy: by keeping interest rates higher than they would otherwise have been; and by sustaining your huge trade deficit – so prompting protectionist pressures to control or stifle imports into the United States. It would be ironic if, at the very moment when the Soviet Union and the East European countries are moving very tentatively towards a loosening of economic controls, the United States economy were to move in the opposite direction.

'Politicians in democracies have a great responsibility to resist the siren calls from special interest groups to interfere with the market in this way: trade unions, farmers, industrialists, public employees. Groups such as these can often whip up public opinion in their favour: accusations of foreign cheating appeal to the narrow-minded streak in all of us – and each intervention seems to cost the individual voter very little. But if these pressures are not resisted – and only politicians can resist them – then loss of freedom and increasing economic sclerosis are the inevitable results. There are plenty of good short-term arguments against protectionism: it puts up prices; it reduces growth at home and overseas; it will make the international debt problem impossible to solve. But in the end the fundamental argument against protectionism (and all forms of intervention in the market) is that it destroys choice and perverts democracy. Free trade is good for all.'

When Sir Geoffrey first moved into the Foreign Office from Downing Street after the 1983 election, he set in hand a complete review of foreign policy objectives. As a result, apart from his vigorous pursuit of the new Europe, his tenure has been very much preoccupied with the attempt to take the chill off East–West relations and to convince the East of the West's constancy and seriousness of purpose. Mrs Thatcher was ready

175

for this change, the more so as her imagination was stirred by brief visits to Moscow for state funerals. Like families, these formal occasions bring leaders together in an atmosphere which underlines the transitoriness of life and can be conducive, if not to philosophical reconciliation, at least to an acceptance that it might be worth seeing if there is any basis for an improvement in relations.

The Foreign Secretary met Andrei Gromyko, then Russian Foreign Minister, a number of times in 1983 and 1984. Mrs Thatcher crossed the Iron Curtain to visit Hungary and openly enjoyed her frank exchange with Mikhail Gorbachev, when he was invited to Britain in 1984 before he became the leader of the Soviet Union. The stage had been set for a diplomatic offensive. Sir Geoffrey went first to Bulgaria and Romania and then in April 1985 to East Germany, Czechoslovakia and Poland. All the time he was pressing the case for human rights. All the time he was expounding the same theme in the same manner, so that the same message reached Moscow ears whether by the backdoor of its associates or through direct contact. He knew what he wanted: balanced, verifiable agreements in a climate of greater confidence and stability. 'We must explain this tirelessly, not just at the negotiating table but in bilateral contacts,' Sir Geoffrey said in his European speech at The Hague in June 1985. 'We must explain it calmly,' he went on. 'Polemics are barren: negotiations must get down to brass tacks. When they do, it will be only the beginning of a very tough process. But at least it will be a beginning. The greatest single gesture it (the Soviet Union) could make to launch a better East–West relationship would be to withdraw its troops from Afghanistan. More generally the Soviet Union must surely see the all-round merits of a more co-operative approach to global problems. We all live in the same world. It will be a safer and more productive world for all of us once the Soviet Union adapts itself, in deeds as well as words, to the complexity of today's international systems, to other regions' rights to free development and to the existence of new challenges that equally affect us all.'

Even the expulsion of a large number of Russians from London in the autumn of 1985 only temporarily refroze the ice. Sir Geoffrey carried on talking and in 1987 made four major speeches on the East–West theme which put his efforts and aspirations in context. 'Good diplomacy relies on a strong bargaining position,' he told the International Institute for Strategic Studies. We cannot ignore 50,000 Warsaw Pact tanks facing Western Europe; 33,000 artillery pieces; 8,000 tactical aircraft; massed divisions of frontline troops; hundreds of thousands of tonnes of chemical weapons; or thousands of nuclear warheads targeted against NATO members. We have just over one-third the number of tanks; less than one-third the artillery; half the aircraft; and virtually no nuclear systems in the short and shorter ranges, where we are outnumbered nine to one. As a defensive alliance, NATO does not need to match the East's arsenal man for man and gun for gun: but we have to state, and face, the facts.

'What does history tell us of Soviet intentions?,' Sir Geoffrey went on. 'How many times in the past two generations have they forcibly imposed their will upon weaker neighbours? Recall the wartime fate of the Baltic states, of Poland and of Finland. Recall the newsreel pictures of Soviet tanks in East Berlin, in Budapest and in Prague. Recall the political and military pressure brought to bear on Poland in 1981 to crush a spontaneous mass movement of ordinary working people. Even today, over 100,000 Soviet troops are massed against the suffering people of Afghanistan. How can we be sure that Soviet leaders will never use their forces against the West? Or try to blackmail us with the threat of these forces, getting their way without firing a single shot? Of course the Soviet Union, like any other sovereign state, is entitled to defend itself. But we are bound to ask why the Soviet military posture in Europe is so dominated by offensive weapons – tanks and bombers, ballistic missiles and chemical weapons? Why is so much of it ranged along the narrow front dividing the two parts of Germany? Why does Soviet doctrine lay so much emphasis on pre-emption? Why do the weapons and military doctrine match so closely what is needed for a swift, offensive strike against Western Europe? Why, in short, do the forces of the Soviet Union go so far beyond the needs of a purely defensive strategy?

'The Soviet Union has vast forces pointed firmly in our direction. And the record shows that it has been ready to use its armed might on weaker states when it thinks it in its interests to do so. That is why we need defence ... The West is faced by the Soviet Union's vast nuclear arsenal. The West must therefore have a nuclear capability of its own. This deters any nuclear attack by the Soviet Union and prevents nuclear black-mail. But the West's nuclear weapons have another function too. They impress on the Soviet Union that the West might respond to an unprovoked attack not merely with conventional forces but also with nuclear weapons. We are not committed to using nuclear weapons first. Nor are we committed to using them in any particular circumstances. But we are committed to having the option: an option which reinforces deterrence by making the Russians realize that the costs of attacking the West could be unbearable.

'No one should have any doubt about our ultimate objective. We look for a relationship with the East which is free from threats. But the Communist governments in the Soviet Union and Eastern Europe still see themselves in an antagonistic relationship with Western democracies. The historic values of democracy, freedom and popular choice which we represent, undermine the claims they make for their political system. The anxieties on this score fuel the massive military spending and relentless propaganda. This is the mentality which still divides Europe.'

Arms control, Sir Geoffrey added, could provide both sides with direct political, economic and strategic benefits, the first priority being a reduction in intermediate nuclear forces, the second an agreement to cut the two super-powers' strategic weapons by fifty per cent and thirdly a total ban on chemical weapons. 'We hold out to the Soviet Union and its allies the prospect of a better, safer relationship based not on pipe-dreams or idealized hopes, but on good old-fashioned enlight-ened self-interest,' he concluded.

In Washington in December 1987, President Reagan and Mr Gorbachev signed the INF treaty, agreed in principle to the fifty per cent reduction in strategic weapons and expressed their commitment to negotiation of a verifiable, comprehensive and effective international convention on the prohibition and destruction of chemical weapons. Sir Geoffrey could well feel he had helped smooth the path.

In another of his East–West speeches, given at Chatham House in London and predating the historic meeting by five months, the Foreign Secretary emphasized the need for realism, vigilance and an open mind. 'So long as Marxism–Leninism remains the official creed of the Soviet Union, and so long as it is claimed to have Universal validity, then the West cannot set aside the ideological component in its analysis of Soviet interests and ambitions,' he said. 'And it has to be said, if we are talking of history, that since 1945 there have been many instances where it would appear that the expansion of Soviet interests has ridden on the backs of Marx and Lenin. Can it be surprising therefore that we ask ourselves whether the Soviet Union is a state whose interests and ambitions are to be judged like any other, by power, geography and history; a state with whom the West would have similar problems of coexistence, whether Communist, Tsarist or something else? Or is the Soviet Union different in kind from other governments, driven by an ideological vision of its state interests, of which realpolitik provides only a partial – and inadequate – interpretation?'

He went on: 'What we need now to consider is whether, when Mr Gorbachev offers us "global detente", he is offering us hope or delusion. History does not provide a particularly hopeful prognosis ... The short answer is that you can sign all the documents in the world: but if mutual confidence is lacking, that will gnaw away at the foundations of the most complex structure of treaties and agreements ... The inescapable conclusion to be drawn from an analysis of detente in the 1970s is that the Soviet Union saw it above all – and here I borrow Soviet jargon – as a stage to be exploited as such: a stage in the still-continuing struggle of ideas and systems that will lead to the triumph of Soviet Socialism. That is why detente got a bad name in the West; and why Western leaders who supported it were often charged with gullibility.

'Glasnost is in essence an internal instrument of the leadership. But thankfully it has repercussions in dealing with the West ... Our aim is patiently to influence by spreading knowledge and building contacts – not to subvert. We are not expecting the Soviet leaders to dismantle their system. Our premise must be that the Soviet Union and its European neighbours contain within themselves the potentiality for conducting a more normal relationship with the outside world, and with their own people ... We are not naive. We shall not convert the Soviet leadership. Irreducible differences will remain. But investment in the infrastructure of knowledge and contact can pay a dividend in the easing of tension, the management of differences.'

Sir Geoffrey said there were three key areas of Soviet policy, which would do more than anything else at present to show the world just how serious the intentions of the Soviet leadership were – Afghanistan, arms control and human rights. 'We have no quarrel with the Russian people,' he continued. 'If Mr Gorbachev can better their standard of living, improve their domestic political system, and introduce a more civilized style into Soviet diplomacy which enables East–West relations to be conducted on a more open and rational basis, that will be all to the good.'

The key to Sir Geoffrey's approach to foreign affairs lies in dialogue and contact. It has a value in itself, he believes, for understanding and confidence-building. But, as he said in his speech at The Hague: 'Stating our views and thrashing them out face to face is not as easy as some think. It takes conviction and subtlety as well as patience. But it is far better than the frustrations, fears and misunderstandings that would multiply in a state of non-communication.' The other thing of course is dogged persistence. He will not give up, he will not lose his temper, he will not accept failure, he will be well briefed and he will keep on coming back because he believes that problems can be managed, if not totally solved. Only history will be able to come to a verdict on his efforts. Europe, East–West, the Middle East and South Africa are still very much live issues. 'Whether any or all of these will yield to the process of negotiation, only time will tell,' Sir Geoffrey once said. 'I think my own experience simply leads on to the conclusion that it is possible to achieve some success this way and that it can be quite fun.'

18

The Way Ahead

By the time they reach their early sixties, some men are obviously tired, bored with the daily routine or simply wishing to do other things with their lives. Geoffrey Howe is obviously cast in a different mould. He is still growing in terms of stature, ability and capacity; a man whom history may rank as a reforming Chancellor and one of Britain's greater Foreign Secretaries; a man whom history may, or may not, offer yet more important challenges.

Sir Geoffrey is likely to become a major contender for the leadership of the Tory Party when Margaret Thatcher retires from the leadership. If he was to become Britain's prime minister, his performance at the Treasury and the Foreign Office would create the expectation of a slow start with a good deal of criticism and that he would then settle down to steer government and the country with increasing confidence. His style is totally different from the present incumbent. Where she might argue, he would probably tend to search for areas of agreement. He is above all a man interested in reconciliation, one who believes it must be possible to manage, if not solve, problems and someone who inspires affection as well as respect. Yet his quiet, reasonable manner conceals radical ideas and a determination to achieve change. While Sir Geoffrey has always been more interested in substance than presentation, his low-key approach has itself reduced potential opposition until repeated exhortation and explanation begins to carry the day. It is one of the odd attributes of Howe's reputation as a mild, amiable politician that his more radical texts are ignored. It remains strange that this Welshman should be so lacking in public passion. He also lacks the obvious vanity and jealousy of most leading men in this field and his self-effacing language is but a token of the attractive modesty of the personality. Apart from the vilification of the trade unions during the Heath Government, Howe has never generated any hostility or venom. His wavelength is so long, he himself is so cautious and his argument so defies abbreviation that the press, let alone people at large, rarely pick up the clarity and uncautious nature of his vision.

What then are his aims for Britain, aims which he will undoubtedly seek to promote for as long as he continues in his present role as Foreign Secretary (which he undoubtedly enjoys), or any other, should the occasion arise. He has given some clues as to the direction the country might take, including speeches to the London School of Economics Conservative Association and the Selsdon Group in 1986 and more recently in a letter to his constituency chairman just before Christmas 1987; a traditional method for ensuring publicity for potentially controversial views.

To the LSE he said: 'The agenda for the future requires tenacity of purpose. The agenda for the last twenty years has been largely shaped by those of us who have worked on the substance of policy, not merely trifling with presentation. The programme first identified by the early Bow Group generations and subsequently filled out and developed by organizations like the Institute of Economic Affairs, remains at the heart of the agenda Britain still needs to carry through. It is no short-term swing of the pendulum. It is the progressive vision of a free, responsible and prosperous society which will call for years more of determined effort.'

To his constituency he wrote: 'We have come a long way over the last eight years but we have still a long way to go in tackling social tensions; tensions caused by generation gaps, racial differences, class and regional divergencies.'

Sir Geoffrey believes that the ground of future political debate will lie not in the principle but in the management of the market economy and the ability of consumers to influence that market and society, including the operation of public services, through increased freedom of choice. He also believes other less materialistic influences need to be brought to bear to affect the way the market economy is managed. 'That means debating not only our economic performance but also the social and moral context within which the market operates,' he wrote. 'These are among the most challenging issues we must tackle: standards, quality, respect for each other – the whole basis for a law-abiding tolerant and peaceful society.' A major objective must be 'to overcome the still too prevalent "chipped white cups of Dover" mentality in public services'. Once people can exert choice within public-sector provision, such as education, health and housing, they can press for higher standards. At the moment these are simply not in keeping with British achievements worldwide.

Howe's enduring revulsion at middle-class intellectual and left-wing illusions about the benevolent state is a strand that runs through from his earliest writing and speeches. 'They simply do not grasp that creativity and dynamism come from individuals not from national plans and that compassion exercised only through the State fails to tap the deep-rooted caring and charitable instincts of the British,' he told the Selsdon Group.

He has also long been concerned about the lack of focus for responsibility in over-powerful nationalized industries which are irresponsive to public pressure and make policy decisions in headquarters remote from management and direct contact with the customer or client. The same problems can occur in monopolies and Geoffrey Howe is now concerned to ensure that future privatization does not fall into this trap. He would also wish to see professions as well as business opened up to the cleansing breeze of increased competition.

'We must seek to break down the barriers of segregation and demarcation which allow us to believe that the State, the social worker or the institution is our brother's keeper,' he said on the same occasion.

Privatization during the Thatcher years may have started out as a somewhat incohate policy to raise money to allow for tax reductions. Now however it has become a coherent

attempt to spread ownership of capital in industry and therefore Britain's future, following in much the same pattern as
home ownership. Howe takes real pleasure in the fact that
in 1979, at the beginning of the Thatcher Government, there
were only thirty employee share-ownership schemes. Just on
ten years later there are 2,000. He is concerned that so many
people are still locked out of participation or ownership. 'Capitalism's benefits have to be shared,' he says. It is likely that
Geoffrey Howe would find some way of ending tax subsidies
for home ownership and affect the balance and fairness of treatment of homes for sale and the rented sector. He acknowledges
that an open market in renting would suit many households
and, to judge from his thinking on housing some thirty years
ago, would probably wish to see the rented market in all but
areas with greatest shortages, equally free of restrictions apart
from freedom of contract.

So far as education is concerned, he wants mainline education to be devolved from the state and local authorities to
schools and parents. In the longer term education may be
funded by the State but only to empower families to choose
the style and nature of schooling they prefer, which implies
variety in content and size. Repayable student loans are likely
for those who go on to higher education. Until recently the
National Health Service, the putative envy of the world, has
been a no-go area for Conservative politicians. Yet throughout
his career Geoffrey Howe has criticized the monopoly nature
of the clinical services of doctors and hospitals. Since the 1960s,
when such an opinion was profoundly risky, he has said that
financial responsibility should be devolved to the local health
authorities and then on to patients. Once the customer can
choose, then workers in the system would need to respond
and enjoy greater control over their own destiny instead of
relying on the present inheritance of management and trade
union confrontation alternating with tussles for more government cash. In the longer term the private sector is likely to
grow with the public acting as a procurer of services rather
than providing everything itself.

Geoffrey Howe sees the problem of the inner cities in a wider
context than mere concern about their potential as flashpoints
for racial riots and civil disturbance. For him the rule of law

must be matched by equal opportunities. 'The challenge of responding to the problems of law and order without abandoning the best aspects of social reform, of combating moral nihilism without resorting to the imposition of our values on others, of retaining a cohesive nation while cherishing the rights of those who want to be different,' he wrote in a pamphlet on policies for the 1980s.

Howe sees Britain awakening from the long enchantment of Socialism. The left held the intellectual initiative for a century and the political policy initiative for fifty years. He believes that this has evaporated since 1979, not simply because of the blunt failure of Socialism to enhance lives and prosperity. The climate of ideas has now moved subtly but profoundly against the whole notion that national plans and rational design are better than the piecemeal, untidy but evolutionary nature of the liberal open society.

A Conservative Britain in the years ahead would have its windows of trade and commerce open to the world. Freer trade will make for easier relations with the East and Islamic countries. Europe would not become some super-state but remain a *Zollverein* with few internal customs formalities for people or goods and so match the United States–Canada, Japanese–Asian and Chinese trading blocks. The United Kingdom would enjoy huge dividends from its accelerating foreign investments. The British capital markets, as the least regulated by nationalistic regulations, could well be the largest in the world. The remaining nationalized industries would be sold on the stock market or to their work forces. State institutions like the BBC would be competing in open markets.

In foreign affairs the search for a positive peace would continue. 'A positive peace in Europe – the peace of the future – would release great energies for both East and West,' Sir Geoffrey said in Berlin in 1984. 'The European Community and the European Free Trade Association together form a mighty free trade area. Western Europe has cornered nearly a third of the world's trade. Imagine what we could achieve if the markets of East and West were also opened up to each other, exposed to the stimulus of genuine competition and development? We would have the resources, not just to co-operate with each other but to confront the new generation of problems in the world at large; to tackle the threats, like terrorism and regional instability; to combat hunger and poverty; to exploit the opportunities of new technology, research and industrial collaboration; to meet the challenges of educational and social change.'

He stresses the importance of effective teamwork as well as a capacity to challenge. 'Our partners are often chosen for us by geography and history and those factors permit no divorce,' he said in his constituency letter. 'In advancing our objectives and defending our interests – whether in Europe, South Africa, the Middle East or elsewhere – we have to maximize all our resources for influence. Friendships new and old; cultural links; the English language; our external broadcasting services; our aid policy; our active role in international financial institutions; the United Nations; collaborative ventures in high technology. All these are pieces of the jigsaw of foreign policy.

'We will fight the next election on our record, as governments must. But that will not be enough. There will be many ready to proclaim the end of an era, to say that the Conservative revolution has served its purpose, to argue that it's time for a change. We must proclaim our vision of a self-confident but not over-confident Britain in the 1990s. A nation with a political culture which values self-reliance above state dependence. A society where growing national wealth can secure essential services for those who need them at standards matching the best in the world. Today's industries and services require, and in the future will increasingly demand, a range of flexibility and adaptability far beyond anything we have yet achieved. It will be the Conservative task to reconcile these pressures, to establish the responsibility which goes with freedom, while ensuring that our society remains open to change.'

To sum up his views is difficult, in part because of his liking for reasoned argument rather than headline-catching clarion calls. However, he undoubtedly wants to see a Britain which is more law abiding and combines greater prosperity and tolerance with a less scruffy appearance. He would hope that renewed economic dynamism and vitality would reach all points of the country. Market forces could thus increasingly provide the framework for activities of all kinds, subject only to key, strategic decisions by government. The tax system would be simplified still further, as would the law – but operate with less discretion within set rules. Any reorganization of the social services and education would aim to give the consumer – patients and pupils (in other words, parents) freedom of choice. There would be scope for a much greater variety of management practice in schools and hospitals, as is the case in business. Teachers, doctors, nurses and other National Health Service staff would be able to exert more influence on their immediate working environment and its services.

In the British Isles, Sir Geoffrey would hope the British and Irish could learn to live alongside one another as comfortably as the French and the Germans. In Europe he would be working for an increasingly united approach in international as well as economic and social affairs – but without diluting the pride, creative strength or character of individual member countries. In the world at large he would continue the present dialogue between East and West aiming to manage problems, reduce tension and so increase freedom of exchange – trade, travel and communications – that both sides would begin to believe the situation would last. He would also undoubtedly, regardless of the political spectrum of the country concerned, continue to press for individual human rights.

Geoffrey Howe is regarded in the parliamentary party as a safe pair of hands. He is liked and trusted across the Tory Party as a whole and wins long ovations for his conference speeches. Like almost all politicians he would like to become prime minister. If he does get the chance, his style would be very different from that of Mrs Thatcher and he would certainly try to reconcile sources of conflict within and without the Party. But there would be no easing of the pressure for change. Indeed, it would seem his perception of Britain's need for change and his belief that he is well equipped to achieve that change is perhaps the mainspring of his political motivation. He is quite revolutionary – but a quiet revolutionary withal.

Index